BUILT

PERTH

DISCOVERING PERTH'S ICONIC ARCHITECTURE
TOM MCKENDRICK AND ELLIOT LANGDON

 FREMANTLE PRESS

CONTENTS

In the relatively short space of time since the Swan River Colony was established, Perth has transformed from a group of tents into a thriving and diverse city. Architecturally, it has faced the challenge of breaking free from the early British-inspired colonial works and developing an identity of its own, specific to the city's unique climate and location. Today, Perth plays host to many exceptional architects and architectural studios, delivering nationally and internationally acclaimed buildings. The city also boasts a high number of important heritage works, and though many of these older buildings have been lost over the years, the state's Heritage Council has worked hard to provide protection for those that remain.

Built Perth is a celebration of architecture in Perth, both new and old, parading the city's most prized architectural works and showing the exciting direction the built environment is taking. For those visiting the city, it provides a selection of noteworthy buildings, from Perth's humble beginnings in convict-built structures, through to innovative modern-day designs. For those living

in Perth, the book is a gentle tap on the shoulder, a finger which points upwards and provides a reminder of the great buildings which surround us, in a city whose architecture has often faced criticism, but which is now pushing forward and turning heads in the world of design.

On the following pages, you'll find 50 of what we believe to be the city's most iconic works of architecture, each one represented in the form of a lovingly crafted illustration. The accompanying text provides key insight into the buildings' histories, uncovering some of the lesser known secrets of the structures of Perth, the clients who commissioned them, the architects who designed them and the various obstacles and triumphs they faced along the way. For each entry, we have included details of the designers, clients, completion dates, costs and styles of the buildings where they are known. Especially with the older buildings, many additions and significant restorations have been done over the years, so this information reflects only the original or most significant contributions. The costs are as accurate as possible, but

can only serve as a guide because many of the records are incomplete or not public information.

To produce a 'Top 50' of the best buildings on offer in Perth is a near impossible task, and in *Built Perth* we do not seek to accomplish any such goal; rather it is a showcase of the vast array of exciting architecture within the coastal city. Whittling the selection down to 50 worthy buildings to research and illustrate turned out to be a harder task than first imagined – we felt spoiled for choice. Firstly, our selection was based loosely on the International Council on Monuments and Sites (ICOMOS) Burra Charter for determining cultural significance, being that each building must have aesthetic, historic, scientific, social or spiritual value for past or present generations. Secondly, we wanted to capture a variety of architecture, in terms of buildings' use, style and age. Lastly, we chose architecture that we love and felt excited to write about, illustrate and share with you. We believe that all are important and have earned their place on the pages of *Built Perth*.

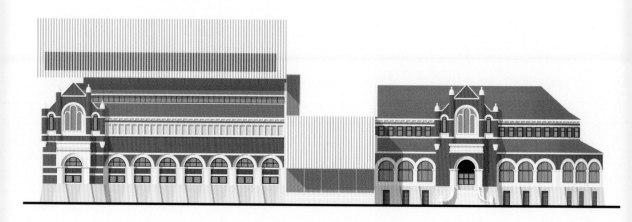

WESTERN AUSTRALIAN MUSEUM

PERTH CULTURAL CENTRE, NORTHBRIDGE

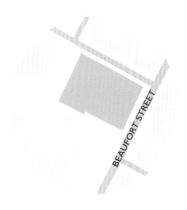

Built in 1856 and originally fronting Beaufort Street, the diminutive form of the Old Perth Courthouse and Gaol set a precedent for its future neighbours, which would also be shaped by some of the state's most renowned names and push architectural boundaries of their time. Richard Roach Jewell designed the limestone jail to show a level of detail and sensitivity not previously seen in colonial architecture, given the basic materials available. After serving its purpose of housing convicts, the building was established as a geological museum in 1891, before being renamed as the Perth Museum the following year.

The prosperity of the gold rush prompted a design to be drawn up for the first dedicated building to house the state's library, art gallery and museum. Famed architect George Temple Poole was to design the scheme, originally envisioning the building to run the full length of the block. Unfortunately, the only portion of his design to ever come to fruition is the Jubilee building on the corner of James and Beaufort streets. The following years saw new homes built for both the art gallery and the library, located in and around their previous location. The Victoria Library lay to the west of the Jubilee building until its demolition in 1985 and a gallery, designed by John Grainger and Hillson Beasley, provided a new frontage to Beaufort Street. While the new gallery followed an aligned material palette, Poole was critical of both buildings for their deviation in style from his original work. Beasley's later design of Hackett Hall in 1913 shares many of the characteristics of the Jubilee building; though due to a falling out between the two architects, it was built deliberately off-centre and short of Poole's work. The gap was filled in 1999 with a modern steel and glass foyer.

Running in the theme of architectural all-stars, Perth now welcomes in the $395.9 million museum addition, a collaboration involving world-renowned architecture firms OMA and HASSELL. The enormous development, floating around and above the existing buildings, unites the site's current heritage works and increases the current museum size fourfold. The bold design seeks to further ignite the already thriving Perth Cultural Centre, with expansive internal galleries to provide a fitting home for the state's treasures.

WESTERN AUSTRALIAN MUSEUM

ARCHITECT
George Temple Poole (Jubilee building); HASSELL and OMA (new addition)

CLIENT
Government of Western Australia

YEAR OF COMPLETION
1897; 2020 (est.)

COST
Unknown; $395.9 million (est.)

STYLE
Federation Romanesque; Twenty-first Century Postmodernist

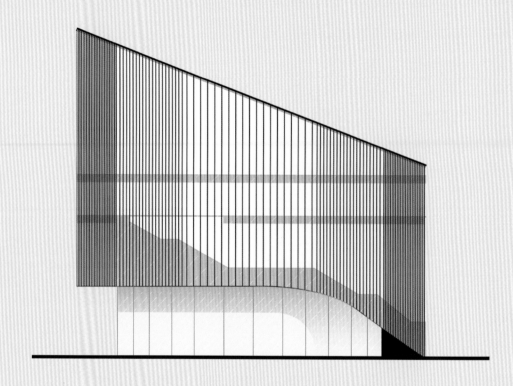

CITY OF PERTH LIBRARY

573 HAY STREET, PERTH

HAY STREET

The first civic building to be constructed by the City of Perth since the Perth Concert Hall in 1973, the City of Perth Library was awarded the coveted George Temple Poole Award in 2016 alongside the neighbouring State Buildings.

The outcome of a national competition, the design of the library complements the composition of the heritage buildings that make up the Cathedral Square precinct and balances them visually. There is a certain poetry in the juxtaposition of the chamfered cylindrical library, the ornate rectilinear Treasury buildings, the pointed facades of the cruciform of St George's Cathedral, and the perfectly manicured landscape that separates them, as if the area had been arranged by Kandinsky himself. The four kilometres of vertical granite-clad 'cassettes' that make up the facade are a superbly contemporary application of an ancient material that might have been used to build the library a century earlier. The entrance foyer and interior are covered in Australian timbers – blackbutt, southern blue gum, spotted gum and Victorian ash – all of which create an interior that is warm and comforting. The sensation of standing inside the library is truly unique: 360 degrees of natural light bathes the timber-laden circular atrium, at the top of which lies the mural *Delight and Hurt Not* by local artist Andrew Nicholls, depicting the final scene of Shakespeare's *The Tempest*. The fairytale at the city's 'lounge room' is topped off by 'the tree of knowledge', a large, live weeping fig on its top floor. With 360 degrees of windows offering priceless views of the nearby heritage buildings to settle next to, the library is an achievement in creating an invaluable sense of community within an urban setting.

ARCHITECT
Kerry Hill Architects

CLIENT
City of Perth

YEAR OF COMPLETION
2016

COST
$60 million

STYLE
Twenty-first Century Organic/Contemporary

PERTH TOWN HALL

CORNER HAY STREET AND BARRACK STREET, PERTH

HAY STREET

PERTH TOWN HALL

With a 38-metre fairytale tower, the Perth Town Hall was built on the highest point in the centre of town, on the approximate location that the first tree was felled nearly 50 years prior to mark the foundation of the colony. It is unlike any other Australian capital town hall, its design akin to public buildings of fourteenth to sixteenth century European villages: a marketplace beneath a hall and clock or watch tower. It is the only town hall in Australia to be built by convicts, with tales long told of subtle nods to the workforce made by the architect in the broad arrow-shaped windows on the tower (a symbol used on convict uniforms) and an architrave in the shape of a hangman's rope. Though it makes for a good yarn, the broad arrow was probably used as it was a symbol that denoted government property.

In the days when the correct time was a privilege affordable only to the wealthy, clock towers were critical to prosperous towns and traditionally placed in the north-west corner of the building with faces in the directions of the compass to help travellers orient themselves. The Perth Town Hall clock has been lovingly cared for by the Ennis family since 1931, who have personally ensured the clock chimes at midnight each new year and that it falls silent for the eleventh hour every Remembrance Day.

The Town Hall's undercroft has provided a setting for a number of uses over time: a market for its first few years, an early fire brigade for the city and shops from the 1920s. The arches were largely removed in favor of steel beams to form shopfronts in the 1920s, before being reinstated nearly 80 years later in 2005. Today the main hall hosts a range of public events from balls and fundraisers to weddings and concerts.

ARCHITECT
Richard Roach Jewell with James Manning

CLIENT
British War and Colonial Office

YEAR OF COMPLETION
1870

COST
£4,600

STYLE
Victorian Free Gothic

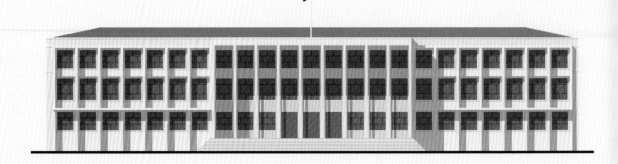

PARLIAMENT HOUSE

4 HARVEST TERRACE, WEST PERTH

The foundation stone for Parliament House was laid in 1902 at the north-eastern corner of the site and, though part of the building was completed in 1904, the stone would remain the sole reminder of the site's original intentions for some sixty years. This tale of two buildings began with a national architectural competition for the design of Perth's Parliament House at the turn of the century. The chosen adjudicator of the competition never selected a winner from the entries, but the project eventually fell to the Public Works Department's chief architect – John Grainger. Grainger's original design underwent a hefty cost-cutting exercise, resulting in a very modest reflection of the intended building. Aside from the legislative assembly and legislative council chambers, the original building contained little else.

While the 1902 design catered for the requirements of parliamentary meetings, by 1950 the need for additional space for staff had become a major issue. Another ongoing point of contention with the design was its orientation, facing west, away from the city, while its eastern facade consisted of a rather inadequate combination of brick and corrugated metal. When Queen Elizabeth II had to be escorted through the tradesmen's entrance to attend a garden party during her visit in 1954, it became clear that it was time to tackle the unrealised eastern wing. In 1964, the east-facing facade, comprising of some 1,500 tonnes of Donnybrook stone, was finally completed at a cost of £416,000. The addition was not designed with grandiose Victorian characteristics as originally intended, instead taking on a more contemporary Stripped Classical style, giving Parliament House its two-faced personality. Aside from providing additional space and modernising the building, the true merit of the new work was that it reoriented the building to face the city so that it now stared straight down St Georges Terrace. This long-awaited focal adjustment was summed up perfectly by an article in the *Sunday Times* featuring the headline, 'A Real Front Door at Last!'

PARLIAMENT HOUSE

ARCHITECT
John Harry Grainger (original building); E.H. Van Mens (1964 addition)

CLIENT
Government of Western Australia

YEAR OF COMPLETION
1904; 1964 (further additions made in 1978, 2002)

COST
£35,600; £416,000

STYLE
Federation Classical; Late Twentieth Century Stripped Classical

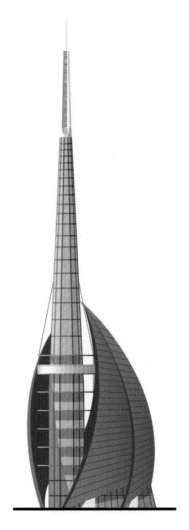

THE BELL TOWER

BARRACK SQUARE, RIVERSIDE DRIVE, PERTH

The image of the 82.5-metre Bell Tower sitting serenely on the bank of the Swan River has become synonymous with Perth. The story of the tower's inception is a somewhat turbulent one, beginning with a gift from England in the form of some very large and very old bells.

In the late 1980s, Western Australia was gifted the twelve bells of St Martin-in-the-Fields in Trafalgar Square, London, where they had been rung for many historic events over hundreds of years. Unfortunately Western Australia had no buildings large enough to house the bells, so they were put into storage where they would remain for the next ten years. Some in England didn't think much of their ancient gift being treated in such a way, sparking a petition in the early 1990s to have the bells brought back to the motherland. This public pressure resulted in a competition for a millennium project as part of the Barrack Square redevelopment to give the bells a permanent home.

A public works project as important as the Bell Tower required a vision for the future, which many people at the time did not share. The initial design came under huge public scrutiny for being both a waste of money and an architectural eyesore. Construction workers reported that in the early stages of the project, cars would stop at the site to provide some well-considered words about the building.

As the tower took shape, the public's criticism died off and their focus could turn back to the design of one of the world's largest musical instruments. The site on Barrack Street was formerly a place of boatbuilding, and the tower heavily reflects this nautical theme. The large copper sails are not only a testament to Perth's connection with the water, but also with the state's mining history. The historic bells sit comfortably at precisely the same height they were once hung in London. Above them is the tower: lightweight, modern and technologically advanced, designed to showcase the engineering capabilities of Western Australia and encapsulate the feeling of a state looking to the future.

THE BELL TOWER

ARCHITECT
Hames Sharley

CLIENT
Government of Western Australia

YEAR OF COMPLETION
2000

COST
$6.8 million

STYLE
Deconstructivist

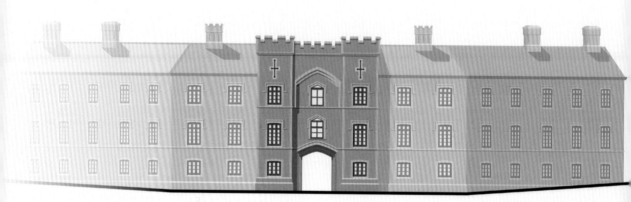

BARRACKS ARCH

CORNER ELDER STREET AND MALCOLM STREET, PERTH

Unbeknown to many locals who aren't old enough to remember, the Barracks Arch that bookends the western end of St Georges Terrace wasn't always a disembodied gateway to the Mitchell Freeway. The crenelated arch, once somewhat generously referred to as Perth's 'Arc de Triomphe', was originally a grand gateway to the Pensioner Barracks that housed the Enrolled Pensioner Force who came to Perth as guards on convict ships. Together with their families, the pensioner guards occupied the barracks until the early 1900s, when it was gradually converted to government offices.

When the eastern wing of Parliament House was added in the 1960s, it became apparent that there was a great barracks-shaped elephant in the room that was blocking the view down St Georges Terrace. Recommendations made in the infamous Stephenson–Hepburn plan of 1955, which shaped Perth from colonial town to the city we know today, called for the complete demolition of the 'inadequate and obsolete building'. The government announced its plans to demolish the building in favour of a new freeway. They were not expecting the public furore that was to follow. The Barracks Defence Council was formed, thousands of signatures

filled petitions, and there was even a plan for a protest in the form of a procession of cars cunningly dubbed a 'Barrackade'. A few days after the planned protest, a group of some 300 University of Western Australia students 'stormed the barracks' in colonial attire as part of the university's infamous annual Prosh Day fundraiser.

The protests and public outrage led to the salvation of the now iconic archway, with the rest demolished to make way for the Mitchell Freeway interchange. Ironically, even with most of the building gone, the disembodied Barracks Arch still perfectly blocked the view down St Georges Terrace from Parliament house – almost comically so, like the leaf on the Statue of David. A number of proposals have been tabled since 1988 to connect the arch to Parliament House with a public-focused 'lid' over the freeway, having the potential to reconnect the city to its estranged neighbour. Sadly for one reason or another the idea has never been realised, but it has re-emerged recently as part of the future master plan for the Parliamentary Precinct. Today the Barracks Arch stands as a testament to the collective will to protect our architectural heritage, a symbol of the birth of architectural conservation awareness in Perth.

MALCOLM STREET

BARRACKS ARCH

ARCHITECT
Richard Roach Jewell

CLIENT
British War and Colonial Office

YEAR OF COMPLETION
1866

COST
£6,700

STYLE
Victorian Tudor

CITY BEACH SURF CLUB

181–183 CHALLENGER PARADE, CITY BEACH

The Perth coastline is littered with world-class beaches, though for over half a century Scarborough and Cottesloe Beaches have stood out as the undisputed homes of beachside hospitality. Partly thanks to Christou Design Group's winning proposal in a national design competition for a new City Beach Surf Club, there is now a third contender on this list. Despite its proximity to the Perth CBD, City Beach feels like a much more serene location than Cottesloe or Scarborough, isolated from the hustle and bustle by an expanse of sand dunes. It was vital that any new development protect this serenity, prompting Christou to design with three objectives in mind: to create a place that celebrates the site and enhances the public experience of our coastline, to create a series of layered buildings which unfurl as you transition from car park to the water's edge, and to create a modest architecture that sits within the landscape without overpowering it. Their proposal pushed the envelope of the brief, adding to it the public space that is now so highly valued to the local community.

Upon arrival at Challenger Parade, visitors are greeted by a handful of high-quality food and beverage offerings in the form of three modern stone-clad pavilions, each divided by a laneway that accesses the main public open space. The two linear built forms of the restaurant precinct and the surf club come together to form a V shape, with the third restaurant pavilion at the interection of the V at the southern point of the site. The space between the buildings is protected from the notorious afternoon blast of south-westerly winds, and is full of sun lounges, lookout points and gathering places, beneath which lies the surf club itself. An amphitheatre, with the stunning backdrop of miles of coastline utopia framed by two mature Norfolk Pines, eases its way down to the beach and surf club, providing the precinct with opportunities for events or civic uses.

When approaching from the beach, the striking stark white nose of the surf club hangs out dramatically; an inviting sense of shelter is evoked when walking beside the 100 metres of gravity-defying wall. The way the building emerges out of the dunes gives it the illusion of being a natural formation. This sensitive design will make the precinct a staple for locals and tourists for years to come.

CITY BEACH SURF CLUB

ARCHITECT
Christou Design Group

CLIENT
City of Perth Surf Life Saving Club

YEAR OF COMPLETION
2016

COST
$17.5 million

STYLE
Twenty-first Century Late Modernist / International

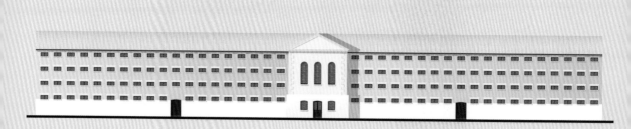

FREMANTLE PRISON

1 THE TERRACE, FREMANTLE

Before becoming the head of the London Metropolitan Police in 1869, Lieutenant-Colonel Sir Edmund Henderson was the first Comptroller-General of Convicts of the newly established penal colony in Western Australia, from 1850 to 1856 and again from 1858 to 1863. He oversaw the construction of cottages for his prison warders and their families between 1851 and 1853 before turning his attention to the convicts, who were still housed in a rented beachside warehouse. Little did he know that 160 years later, his plan for the new prison would become Western Australia's first and only UNESCO World Heritage–listed building and one of its premier tourist attractions.

The chosen site was high on the hill overlooking the town, with a belief that the clean fresh air would aid in the reformation of the inmates and help prevent disease. The site was levelled, with the limestone quarried during site works eventually reused to construct the prison. In 1853, work began on the intimidating six-metre-high perimeter wall, over which a number of prisoners made their break for freedom throughout the prison's history.

Henderson's design for the main cell block was based on London's infamous Pentonville Prison and constructed from locally sourced limestone. The cells finally welcomed in their unenthusiastic inhabitants in 1855, the convicts now finding themselves imprisoned within the cramped cells on which they had laboured. At 150 metres in length, the completed four-storey cell block was the longest in the Southern Hemisphere. Internally, the iron fixings for the doors and gallery balustrades were salvaged from convict ships, with access to the upper levels via a jarrah spiral staircase.

Eighteen years after the last convict ship was unloaded in Western Australia in 1868, only 60 men were left imprisoned under the convict system in Western Australia. The prison was handed over by the British to the colonial Government, and was used to house the state's felons until the infamous 1988 riot ultimately lead to its closure in 1991.

Since its closure, Fremantle Prison has taken on a very different role and now stands as one of Western Australia's premier tourist attractions. Complete with a museum and various guided tours, visitors flock to be taken through the country's largest and most intact convict-built prison.

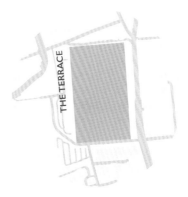

FREMANTLE PRISON

ARCHITECT
Edmund Yeamans Walcott Henderson

CLIENT
British War and Colonial Office

YEAR OF COMPLETION
1859

COST
£8,000 (main cell block)

STYLE
Colonial Georgian

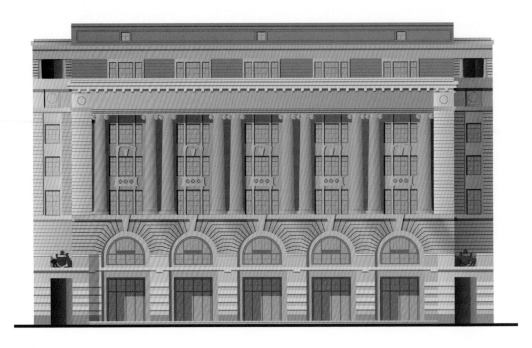

PERTH GPO

3 FORREST PLACE, PERTH

Our overwhelming desire for communication has, in the past, seen post offices given high favour in any new town or colony. For the most isolated city in the world, communication was especially important, and Perth's former general post offices now stand as some of the city's most treasured heritage works. George Temple Poole's beautiful design on St Georges Terrace was completed in 1890, and played its role well for a time, but by 1910 it was clear that building was no longer sufficient. The rapidly growing city saw its population triple from 1890 to 1900, in part due to interstate migration following the collapse of the Melbourne land boom and financial unrest in other colonies.

The new GPO building in Forrest Place served its original purpose as Perth's central post office for 93 years. Construction began in 1914, but the outbreak of World War I delayed work significantly, with the steel intended for use in the GPO being redirected to the war effort. Upon its completion on 26 September 1923, the *West Australian* described it as 'the most sumptuous and impressive Federal building in Australia'. In 2016 the post office closed to become the home of a Swedish fashion retailer.

If you look closely you will notice the kangaroo on the coat of arms is looking over its shoulder rather than towards the crest as is customary. Local legend has it that the sculptor, suspicious that the government might neglect to pay him due to the construction delays, turned the kangaroo's head towards the Treasury building as a warning. A far more likely, though mundane, reason is that the kangaroo and emu were cast with turned heads to look towards the English coat of arms and that, unaware of this, the contractors mounted them on the wrong side of each other, though this has never been confirmed.

PERTH GPO

ARCHITECT
Hillson Beasley and
John Smith Murdoch

CLIENT
Government of Western
Australia

YEAR OF COMPLETION
1923

COST
£400,000

STYLE
Federation Beaux Arts

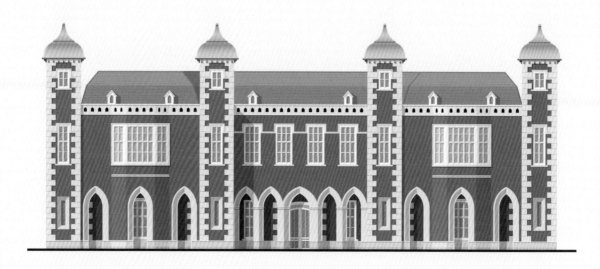

GOVERNMENT HOUSE

13 ST GEORGES TERRACE, PERTH

Three governors' residences came and went before the picturesque old English mansion that is the current Government House was built. The first was a series of tents set up on Garden Island in 1829 upon the arrival of the first settlers, followed closely by a wooden hut located in what is now Stirling Gardens. The first house of any substance was designed in 1834 by civil engineer Henry Reveley under instruction from Governor James Stirling. The resulting Georgian-style building was by all reports entirely inadequate for human occupation. The roofs leaked, the floors were devoured by termites and the design did not allow enough space for entertaining large numbers of guests – an essential function of a governor's accommodation. Despite the poor living conditions, four governors occupied the house before Governor Arthur Kennedy declared the building unacceptable and commissioned a new dwelling to be constructed.

Kennedy never took up residence in the finished house as the construction took several years to complete and the cost spiralled to over double the initial estimate. While convict labour was available, the economic situation of the time meant it was used exclusively for private sector works. In 1863 a convict ship, the *York*, brought in workers applicable for public projects and the sluggish pace of construction began to increase.

Edmund Henderson's design was sure to make its early owners a touch homesick as it harked back to the motherland, from the Flemish bonded brickwork and decorated gables to the arcading at ground level derived from the Fonthill Gothic style, which was popular in England at the time.

The first occupant of Government House was Kennedy's successor, Governor John Hampton, who wasn't entirely content with his new abode. Before the building was complete, Hampton had begun work on alterations to increase the size of the ballroom. He then further irritated the public by spending a substantial amount of money adorning the many rooms (today the building has 41) with exquisite furnishings shipped over from England. While a number of alterations and additions have been made over the years, Government House stands relatively unchanged and has remained the residence of Western Australian governors until the present day.

GOVERNMENT HOUSE

ARCHITECT
Edmund Yeamans Walcott Henderson with James Manning and Richard Roach Jewell

CLIENT
British War and Colonial Office

YEAR OF COMPLETION
1864

COST
£15,000

STYLE
Victorian Tudor

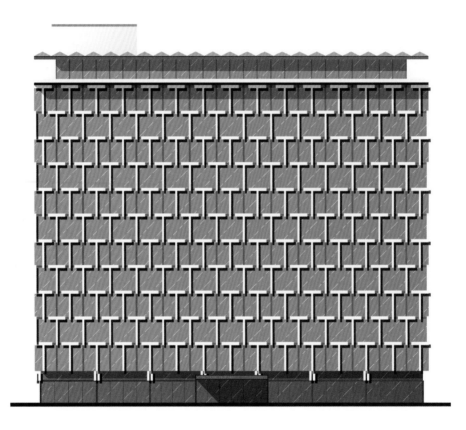

COUNCIL HOUSE

27 ST GEORGES TERRACE, PERTH

Arguably one of the purest examples of Post-war International–style Modernist office buildings in Australia, this one-of-a-kind tower demonstrates a mastery of composition and proportion. Council House was the result of an international design competition held by the City of Perth after it was announced that it would host the next Empire Games in 1962. The competition saw some 61 entrants judged by a panel of jurors including Harry Seidler. Seidler eloquently described Howlett & Bailey's design as 'a remarkably simple solution to a complex problem'. It was the first example of window-walling in Perth, adorned with T-shaped, tiled brise-soleils, and symbolised Perth's transformation into a modern city on an international scale.

Council House was nearly lost in the early 1990s when it was earmarked for demolition by the state government and the City of Perth. Never before had the city seen such uproar and unification over the demolition of a modern building, epitomised by the painting of the slogan, 'If you knock this down, you're a bloody idiot' on the hoardings of the demolition site. The resultant conversation caused Perth to rethink what makes a building worth protecting, and to realise that its significance is determined by more than just its age. Council House was added to the heritage register and underwent a major renovation in 1997 at a cost of $25.3 million. The building was stripped to its bare bones, a process that included removing the seemingly infinite tiny mosaic tiles which cover the T shapes, repairing and re-gluing them.

In 2009, a state-of-the-art LED light system was added to the facade, turning the entire building into a screen visible from Kings Park. The 548 lights change colours and show messages relating to significant events.

COUNCIL HOUSE

ARCHITECT
Howlett & Bailey Architects

CLIENT
City of Perth

YEAR OF COMPLETION
1963

COST
£1.5 million

STYLE
Post-war International

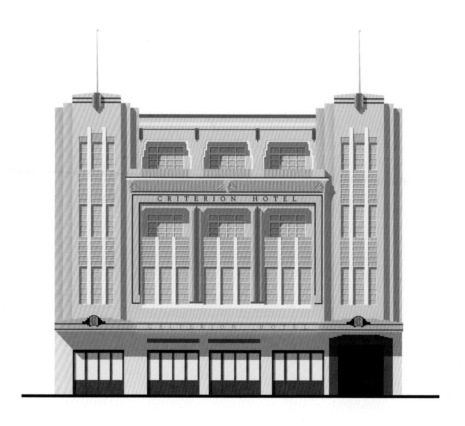

CRITERION HOTEL

560 HAY STREET, PERTH

The beautifully detailed Criterion Hotel is somewhat unassuming, located opposite the new City of Perth Library. One of many great buildings in the CBD that often goes unnoticed above its awning, this historic beauty holds the record for the longest continuously serving licensed premises in Perth, wetting whistles since 1848.

The Criterion, briefly renamed as the Regatta Hotel in the 80s and 90s, is the third building on the site and the second to go by that name. The first building was called the John Bull Inn, and was colloquially referred to as the 'funeral cockpit', due to its role as the last stop for pallbearers and their cargo on the long journey to the cemetery. It was also one of the first establishments in Perth to be serviced with electric lighting, flicking the switch for the first time on a Saturday night in 1892.

The currently standing 1937 Art Deco building was designed by Hobbs, Forbes & Partners for the Swan Brewery Company, with no expense spared to give the building a modern appearance. Furnishings were provided by Boans department store at a cost of over £7,000 and included a luxurious single-pattern carpet, the largest to be laid in Australia at the time. Each of the 74 rooms had natural light and ventilation, most also with their own hot water supply and telephones. Externally, the facade has a symmetrical design, bookended by twin vertically emphasised and stepped towers, each topped with a flagpole – an aesthetic known as 'Skyscraper Style'. Over the years, the hotel has housed a wide range of celebrity guests, from the then soon-to-be thirty-first president of the United States, Herbert Hoover, to local legend Prince Leonard of the Western Australian micronation, the Hutt River Province. Still operating as a hotel, the Criterion is the quirky Art Deco neighbour of the architecturally diverse Cathedral Square Precinct, and remains an everlasting reminder of post-Depression optimism.

CRITERION HOTEL

ARCHITECT
Hobbs, Forbes & Partners

CLIENT
Swan Brewery Co.

YEAR OF COMPLETION
1937

COST
£42,000

STYLE
Inter-war Art Deco

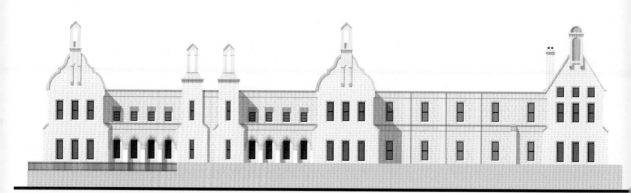

FREMANTLE ARTS CENTRE

1 FINNERTY STREET, FREMANTLE

Viewed as one of Australia's best examples of Colonial Gothic architecture, the Fremantle Arts Centre is certainly one of the port city's best loved buildings. On sunny Sunday afternoons, people flock inside the limestone perimeter walls to sample the delights of the cafe or lounge on its well-kept lawns, serenaded by local live music. The tranquil setting makes it easy to forget the building's chequered past, including its origins as an asylum.

Convicts built the northern wing using hand-split sheoak roof shingles, jarrah floorboards and limestone blocks quarried from the future site of the Fremantle Prison. Later additions, including a wing to the north-east facing Finnerty Street and a number of extensions to the south of the existing work, were designed by George Temple Poole and contracted to the Bunning brothers in the 1880s – one of their early stepping stones in the creation of the now famous Bunnings empire. The Fremantle Lunatic Asylum was opened in 1861 as a place to hide the colony's 'undesirables' from public view. Those housed in the new building included not only the insane but also the impoverished, alcoholics, criminals, sexual deviants or those suffering depression. Conditions in the asylum and the treatment of its occupants were somewhat inhospitable, contributing to the belief by many today that the Arts Centre is Western Australia's most haunted building.

Due to overcrowding, the building was declared unfit for purpose in the early 1900s and was converted into a women's home. While this may conjure up images of charity and care, the home was in essence a prison for those of low social standing – the elderly, unmarried, prostitutes or abandoned women. Eventually a lack of funding and the poor condition of the building saw the women moved to a different facility in the 1920s.

The centre continued its theme of varied use, becoming a US Navy supply depot with the illustrious name 'Depot 137' in 1942, then being converted into a technical college after the war, but by the 1960s the building had fallen into disrepair. Public outcry and Fremantle's mayor at the time, Sir Frederick Samson, saved the building from demolition, and restoration works were carried out using traditional building techniques by Robin McKellar Campbell in 1968.

Today the Fremantle Arts Centre thrives as a hub of activity and the arts, exhibiting the works of local, national and international artists as well as hosting concerts from world-renowned performers.

FINNERTY STREET

FREMANTLE ARTS CENTRE

ARCHITECT
Edmund Yeamans Walcott Henderson (original building); George Temple Poole (later additions)

CLIENT
British War and Colonial Office

YEAR OF COMPLETION
1861; 1894

COST
Unknown

STYLE
Colonial Gothic Picturesque

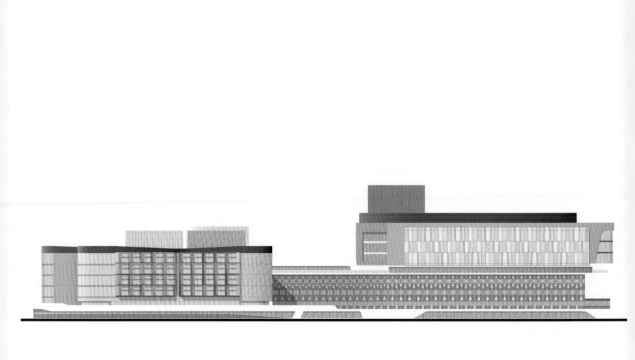

PERTH CHILDREN'S HOSPITAL

15 HOSPITAL AVENUE, NEDLANDS

Despite being marred by a number of issues that caused almost three years of delays, the 298-bed Perth Children's Hospital, built to replace the 109-year-old Princess Margaret Hospital, has proved to be entirely worth the wait. Over 200 design professionals worked on the project, and the State's commitment to delivering a world-class facility will benefit Western Australia's children for years to come.

The inspiration for the building's form and colour palette sits adjacent to the site – Kings Park, Perth's giant urban garden. The shape of the hospital is derived from a flower: the 'stem' begins at the northern end and winds its way south before erupting in a head of 'petals' forming the in-patient wing with views out over the parkland. The design generously delivers natural light to the interior of the building, while the facade adapts to reflect its heat where necessary. A further reference to the park runs along the eastern side of the hospital in the form of *Fizz*, an artwork by Stuart Green consisting of nearly 1,600 coloured circles that reflect the hues and movements of the bushland across the road.

Perhaps the greatest success of the building is its ability to feel entirely unlike a hospital. Every detail has been designed from a child's perspective: seating areas are made for climbing, hiding or indeed sitting, staff stations take on the form of tree houses, lowered window seats allow views to the outside world and coloured ceiling features provide a distraction for patients being wheeled through the corridors. Every inch of the building provides intrigue and distraction from the primary purpose of being inside.

ARCHITECT
Cox Architecture, JCY Architects & Urban Designers, Billiard Leece Partnership and HKS

CLIENT
Government of Western Australia

YEAR OF COMPLETION
2018

COST
$1.2 billion

STYLE
Contemporary

FREMANTLE TOWN HALL

8 WILLIAM STREET, FREMANTLE

The 1870s saw the small coastal colony of Fremantle growing rapidly, with a town council replacing the town trust in 1871. The need for a town hall was raised, but due to immediate concerns for basic public works, this plan was put to bed for ten years. The state's Government Engineer had come up with a design for the building back in 1876, and a subsequent concept submitted by R.B. Lucas in 1881 was initially accepted by the council, who then later changed their mind, opting to go with the design from Melbourne-based architects Grainger and D'Ebro. The triangular site in Kings Square was sold to the council by the Church of England, who intended to build a new St John's Church on its northern portion. Selling off the southern segment provided the church with the necessary funds for their building and furnished the council with the perfect location for their town hall. While the council initially opted for a pared back version of Grainger and D'Ebro's design, a somewhat rare occurrence in a ratepayers' meeting saw a push towards raising additional funds and constructing the design in all its Victorian Classical glory.

To celebrate the opening of the new building and its 32-metre clock tower in 1887, an extravagant ball was arranged, with a children's fancy dress ball scheduled for the following evening. In a strange turn of events, the ball was gatecrashed by a number of unruly characters, led by the landlord of the National Hotel, William Conroy. When denied entry to the party, an enraged Conroy shot the town supervisor, John Snook, who died some weeks later. For this act, Conroy unwittingly claimed the unenviable title of 'last man hanged' in the Perth Gaol.

While the Town Hall remains much the same as when it was first constructed, in 2017 it was the subject of the single largest heritage restoration ever carried out by the City of Fremantle. The $3.1 million restoration involved the removal of decades worth of paint from the stucco walls, reconstruction of the roof forms and restoration of the historic clock. The work was carried out using traditional building methods and materials and received a prestigious Western Australian State Heritage Award in 2018.

WILLIAM STREET

FREMANTLE TOWN HALL

ARCHITECT
John Harry Grainger and Charles D'Ebro

CLIENT
Fremantle Town Council

YEAR OF COMPLETION
1887

COST
£10,800

STYLE
Victorian Free Classical

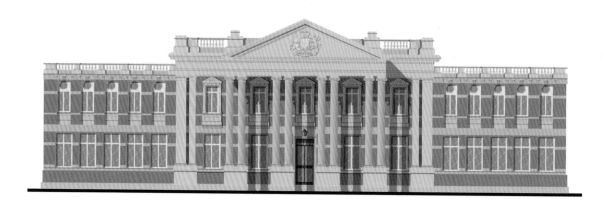

SUPREME COURT OF
WESTERN AUSTRALIA

28 BARRACK STREET, PERTH

The Supreme Court of Western Australia was formed in 1861, with judiciary functions moving from the old Perth Gaol (now part of the Western Australian Museum) back to the colony's first courthouse in what is now Stirling Gardens. The old courthouse still exists adjacent to the Supreme Court building and is the oldest building in Perth, now housing the Law Museum. It is one of two remaining buildings (the other is the Fremantle Roundhouse) designed by the first civil engineer of the Swan River Colony, Henry Reveley.

Life in the courts was a little more tumultuous in the young colony than it is these days, from the first chief justice Archibald Burt having to hold an umbrella during court proceedings because of the leaky roof, to choking out a sentencing in a smoke-filled, albeit warm, courtroom during winter when court was temporarily held in the colony's commissariat stores. Over time, it became apparent that a new courthouse was necessary.

In 1901, the parliament announced that a stately new supreme court would be built of entirely locally sourced materials including Donnybrook stone, jarrah and Meckering granite, though construction would ultimately face a few cutbacks. Unfortunately the Donnybrook quarry began to run dry of consistently coloured product and it was proposed that the stone be substituted with stucco and cement. The decision to use the relatively new technology caused such a media stir that a royal commission was called, which ruled in favour of the stucco and cement substitute that now makes up the grand northern entrance. The specified slate roof was then replaced with a cheaper galvanised iron alternative and the foyer, which was intended by architect John Grainger to be painted in bright colours, was whitewashed, though the original design was eventually realised for the building's centenary in 2003.

The Supreme Court building was considered a technological achievement for its time, due to its construction on reclaimed land that was formerly part of the Swan River foreshore, and its impeccably manicured public gardens that insulate it from the hustle and bustle of the city and differentiate it from other court buildings around the country. Many historic moments have occurred within its walls: the last death sentence in Western Australia was handed down to serial killer Eric Edgar Cooke in this very building in 1963, notorious serial-killing couple Catherine and David Birnie were given life sentences in 1987, and famed businessman Alan Bond was served with jail time for the biggest corporate fraud case in Australian history.

SUPREME COURT OF WESTERN AUSTRALIA

ARCHITECT
John Harry Grainger

CLIENT
Government of Western Australia

YEAR OF COMPLETION
1903

COST
£55,900

STYLE
Federation Academic Classical

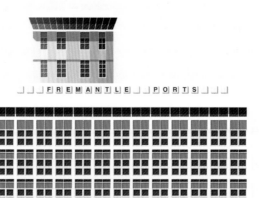

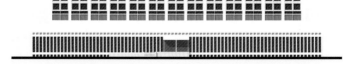

FREMANTLE PORTS
ADMINISTRATION BUILDING

1 CLIFF STREET, FREMANTLE

CLIFF STREET

FREMANTLE PORTS ADMINISTRATION BUILDING

Providing Western Australians with the goods they depend on is a task that falls largely to the port of Fremantle, with around $3 million on average in trade passing through per hour. To facilitate these demands, the port requires a central operational hub, which exists in the form of Fremantle's very own 'skyscraper', the Ports Administration building. To this day, the structure stands as the port city's tallest building, at a lofty 60 metres. Its simple form, rectangular footprint and minimal ornamentation demonstrate a classic example of the International style.

Built by eminent Perth builders A.T. Brine and Sons, the administration building is considered ahead of its time, and not only because of the maritime signalling and navigational technology housed within its walls.

The design takes into consideration the building's orientation on its site to avoid the harsh morning and evening sun, with tinted windows throughout and sun baffles to protect the northern facade. The aluminium-framed windows are all fully reversible to allow for ease of cleaning and the top of the tower's extended rectangular base is made of white folded concrete to control heat gain, which at the time of building was the only example of this technique in Australia.

Atop the eleven-storey rectangular form sits a three-level tower, which houses a signal station. From here, 360-degree, uninterrupted views allow the harbourmaster to keep a close eye on every aspect of port life, ensuring Fremantle's roaring sea trade can continue unhindered.

ARCHITECT
Hobbs, Winning & Leighton

CLIENT
Fremantle Port Authority

YEAR OF COMPLETION
1964

COST
£650,000

STYLE
Post-war International

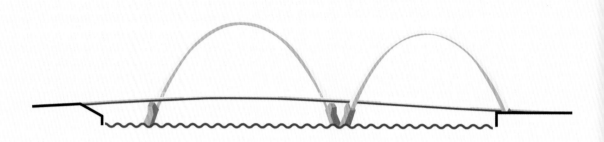

ELIZABETH QUAY BRIDGE

ARUP ASSOCIATES

NARROWS BRIDGE

WILLIAM HOLFORD & PARTNERS

MATAGARUP BRIDGE

DENTON CORKER MARSHALL

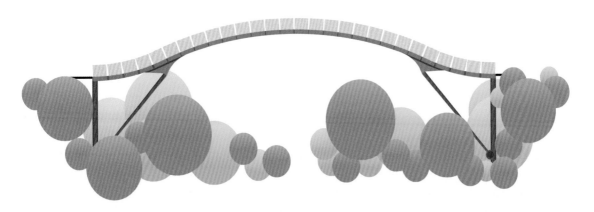

KINGS PARK FEDERATION WALKWAY

DONALDSON + WARN

WEST AUSTRALIAN BALLET
COMPANY CENTRE

134 WHATLEY CRESCENT, MAYLANDS

The former Western Australian Institute and Industrial School for the Blind is a building that is steeped in history. The remaining Art Deco portion of the complex, which was originally founded in 1897, was designed in 1937 by government architect A.E. (Paddy) Clare. Clare is responsible for a number of high-quality government buildings around Perth, including the former Perth Girls School in East Perth and part of King Edward Memorial Hospital in Subiaco.

The building is decorated with Inter-war Stripped Classical and Art Deco detailing: porticos, piers, a defined plinth, and perhaps most notably, the geometric friezes. The Stripped Classical style, as the name suggests, took the shell of a classical building but stripped the classical decorative elements and ornamentations – you will not find Corinthian columns, entablatures or pediments here. It was among the styles that marked the beginning of what we know today as Modernist architecture – adapting the architecture of centuries past, rather than mimicking it.

The industrial school taught skills and provided work and accommodation for the state's blind population: primarily manufacturing cane and wicker furniture, mats and brushes. The institute was quickly realigned to help the war effort following the outbreak of World War II, with workers working ten days for nine days' pay producing nets and baskets, some collapsible to house carrier pigeons, all for the military.

After the end of the war, in 1948, the famous deaf-blind Harvard graduate Helen Keller paid the institute a visit, and was reportedly shocked to discover children were still educated in the fairly archaic industrial environment. She backed a movement to educate the visually impaired in occupations other than manual labour, and throughout the next 50 years the facility was modernised and expanded, before eventually relocating in 2004. The building sat empty until a successful fundraising campaign raised $12 million to restore the building and convert it into a world-class dance facility – now the home of ballet in Western Australia.

WHATLEY CRESCENT

WEST AUSTRALIAN BALLET COMPANY CENTRE

ARCHITECT
A. E. Clare

CLIENT
Government of Western Australia

YEAR OF COMPLETION
1937

COST
£13,400

STYLE
Inter-war Stripped Classical / Art Deco

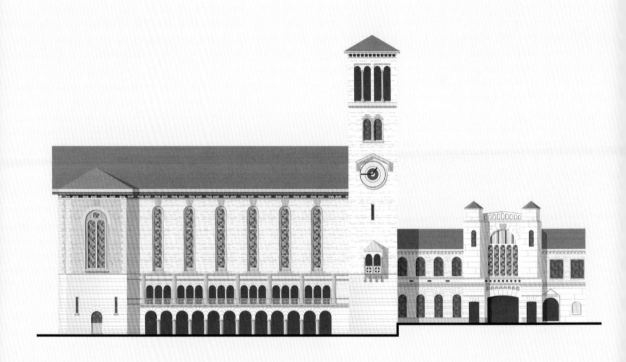

WINTHROP HALL

35 STIRLING HIGHWAY, CRAWLEY

When the University of Western Australia began educating students in 1913, they did so from the somewhat ramshackle 'Tin Pan Alley', so named because the collection of buildings was constructed from corrugated iron, on Irwin Street in the city. There is no doubt that the campus was destined for an upgrade, though it is unlikely that the Ivy-League aesthetic of the campus would exist if it were not for the university's founder, Sir John Winthrop Hackett. Upon his death in 1916, Winthrop Hackett left a bequest of £425,000 to the university, part of which funded the Hackett Memorial Buildings with Winthrop Hall as their centerpiece.

The foundations for Winthrop Hall were laid in 1929 by builder A.T. Brine, after the winning design by Melbourne architects Conrad Sayce and Rodney Alsop was selected from 52 entries. The design originally drew criticism for its Romanesque style, the argument being that Gothic Revival would have been more appropriate for an academic building. On the contrary, the Romanesque style is almost exclusively reserved for architecture of a spiritual nature in Australia and is part of what makes Winthrop Hall such a celebrated and unique building. The facade is made primarily from reinforced concrete and Donnybrook stone that – when combined with the Greek-influenced lion-griffin-spangled frieze, the Italian columns inspired by the Cathedral of Monreale in Sicily, and the Spanish Cordova roof tiles – gives the hall a distinctly Mediterranean appearance. The spectacular original stained glass in the many windows of Winthrop Hall owed their brownish hues to Alsop's innovative scheme to recycle old medicine and beer bottles – a resource that was undoubtedly in no short supply at the blossoming university.

In front of Winthrop Hall sits the reflection pool, designed to give the building the affectation of increased stature. As the opening ceremony for the hall drew near, the pool remained unfinished and the student body jumped to the rescue, providing some last-minute free labour to get construction across the line on time. The pool, which continues to play a part in student life, used to be the battleground for a 'freshers' initiation involving throwing as many students from other faculties as possible into the water. Nowadays, it's more commonly used as the serene backdrop to graduation and wedding photos.

STIRLING HIGHWAY

WINTHROP HALL

ARCHITECT
Rodney Alsop and Conrad Sayce

CLIENT
University of Western Australia

YEAR OF COMPLETION
1932

COST
£250,000

STYLE
Inter-war Romanesque

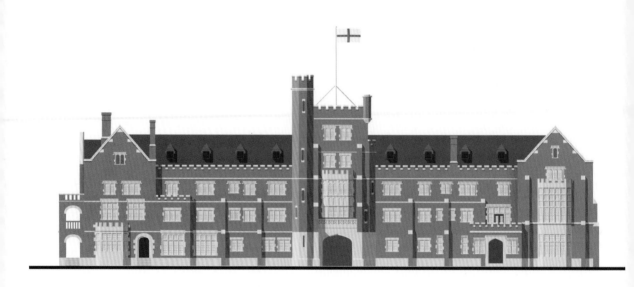

ST GEORGE'S COLLEGE

46 MOUNTS BAY ROAD, CRAWLEY

Set back from the hustle and bustle of Mounts Bay Road, at the end of a great horseshoe driveway, beyond the perfectly manicured gardens and grand old Moreton Bay figs, lies our very own curiously placed slice of Cambridge University. The resemblance to Cambridge's Selwyn College is no coincidence, though the actual intention was that the design would reflect Caius College, where then archbishop Charles Riley had been educated.

When one of the founding fathers of Western Australia's first university passed away in 1916, he bequeathed the hefty sum of £425,000 to the University of Western Australia. Sir John Winthrop Hackett, whose names are found on the two main halls and the two main streets of the university, wished for some of these funds to go towards the construction of an Anglican residential college. The man chosen to design the building was none other than local war hero and 'starchitect' Lieutenant General Sir J. J. Talbot Hobbs. Hobbs, of the firm Hobbs, Smith & Forbes, designed the college in the Tudor Gothic style to resemble an Oxbridge college at

the request of Archbishop Riley, who himself was educated at Cambridge. The college was opened in April 1931 and it was only three years before the first of 25 St. George's residents was selected as a Rhodes Scholar.

The college exclusively accepted male students for 50 years, accepting the first female students in 1981. Many additions to the building over the years have increased the college's capacity to over 200, more than the total number of students who attended the entire university in its first few years. The college is the most traditional on campus, with many strong customs. Until recently, the students had to wear their academic regalia for dinner in the refectory every night, a practice that is now reserved for formal occasions. As a result of their unique shared experiences from living in a college whose grounds and traditions have remained relatively intact, the residents of St George's College are known to form a strong bond during their time there; a bond which is maintained by alumni long after graduation.

ST GEORGE'S COLLEGE

ARCHITECT
Hobbs, Smith & Forbes

CLIENT
University of Western Australia and Perth Diocesan Trustees

YEAR OF COMPLETION
1931

COST
Unknown

STYLE
Inter-war Tudor Gothic

REGAL THEATRE

474 HAY STREET, SUBIACO

'New Subiaco' was founded to the west of the Perth settlement in the mid nineteenth century by Benedictine monks, who named the area after the town in Italy that was the birthplace of their order. The monks moved to greener pastures in New Norcia, but the name stuck and, with the help of a well-placed station on the Perth to Fremantle railway, Subiaco grew into a thriving settlement. The now inner-city suburb catered for work, rest and play for all, from the working class to high society, and the corner of Hay Street and Rokeby Road was the epicentre of entertainment in the area.

The rise of moving pictures saw the creation of the Coliseum Picture Gardens in around 1916 on the future site of the Regal Theatre, opposite the grand Subiaco Hotel. The advent of the sound revolution brought 'the talkies' and a renewed interest in cinema around the time of the Great Depression. It was a chance to temporarily exchange the harsh realities of life at the time for the glitz and glamour of Fred Astaire and Ginger Rogers. The Regal, as well as the Como, Piccadilly, Astor, and Windsor theatres, were designed during this time by specialist cinema architect William T. Leighton, and are still in operation today, though some have been converted to live venues, as the Regal was in 1977.

Named for King George VI, who had recently ascended the throne, the Regal opened to an elated crowd in April 1938 with a double feature screening of *Love Under Fire* and *Shall We Dance* with Fred Astaire and Ginger Rogers. It was designed to reflect the advanced technology and sophistication of the activity it housed: sleek, modern, streamlined, geometric, and with an adoration for the corner – all the hallmarks of an Inter-war Art Deco shrine to the moving picture. The Regal echoes the form of the Subiaco Hotel across the road, with both imposing structures making the most of their prime corner locations, though they are very different stylistically. Upon opening, the theatre seated over 1,000 patrons in the auditorium and dress circle, and included all of the latest amenities – particularly if you were were accompanied by a young child. A soundproof 'crying room' was located at the back of the theatre, so mothers could watch the movie without disturbing others. There were also numbered pram parking bays, where infants could be left to sleep. When they cried, the number of their pram bay would flash on the corner of the screen to alert the relevant parent. Today the theatre attracts thousands per year to see its shows featuring nationally and internationally recognised talent, and shows no sign of slowing down.

HAY STREET

REGAL THEATRE

ARCHITECT
William Garnsworthy Bennett and William T. Leighton

CLIENT
Messrs. Coade and A.T. Hewitt

YEAR OF COMPLETION
1938

COST
£25,000

STYLE
Inter-war Art Deco

HIS MAJESTY'S THEATRE

825 HAY STREET, PERTH

HAY STREET

One of the only examples of Baroque-inspired architecture in Perth, this grand old theatre has hosted performances by the likes of Anna Pavlova, Katharine Hepburn, Barry Humphries and Sir Ian McKellen, to name just a few. 'The Maj', as it is colloquially known, is one of the last operating Edwardian-era theatres left in Australia and one of two remaining 'His Majesty's' theatres left in the world. It was the largest theatre in Australia when it was built during the gold rush for well-to-do businessman and soon-to-be mayor of Perth, Thomas Molloy, boasting an adjoining 65-room hotel that now houses offices and dressing rooms for the resident companies The West Australian Ballet and West Australian Opera.

The theatre was originally capped with a domed roof that slid open to ventilate the auditorium. Four small water features either side of the stage and several fans also helped to counter the heat generated by capacity crowds of up to 2,584 theatregoers on balmy Perth summer evenings. It is said that, at least on one occasion, the open roof provided thunder and lightning special effects on cue during a performance of *A Midsummer Night's Dream* – though the mood was quickly dampened by the following downpour. The dome was permanently sealed when the theatre underwent major renovations after it was acquired by the state government in the late 1970s.

The tremendously ornate two-level cast iron verandah was removed in the late 1940s as its pillars posed a risk to the ever-increasing motor traffic, and constructions like these were liable to fall on pedestrians when their supports were damaged. This explains the lack of ornamentation on the lower stories, as the facade would originally have been hidden from view. Fortunately, there are plans to reinstate the verandah to its former glory in the coming years as part of ongoing heritage works.

HIS MAJESTY'S THEATRE

ARCHITECT
William George Wolfe

CLIENT
Thomas Molloy

YEAR OF COMPLETION
1904

COST
£42,000

STYLE
Federation Free Classical

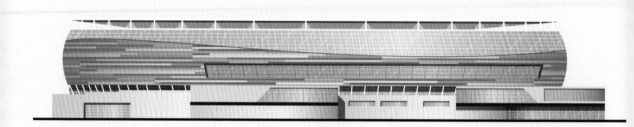

PERTH STADIUM

333 VICTORIA PARK DRIVE, BURSWOOD

Over the past few decades, stadiums have steadily moved from eyesores to city-focused architectural statements, and Perth has eagerly awaited the arrival of its new 60,000 seat sporting venue.

In the only country where four different codes of football are played professionally, and where cricket and live music are popular events, any stadium design would need to show impressive flexibility. Perth Stadium responds to this through its 'bowl' shape and column-free roof structure, providing uninterrupted views from every seat in the house.

Notably absent from the stadium are lighting towers, often a necessary evil that dominate the skyline and detract focus from the building itself. The system illuminating the venue incorporates more than 15,000 LED lights and is the largest of its kind in the world, with the added party trick of putting on dazzling light shows in team colours. The 200 tonnes of anodised aluminium cladding that wrap the external facade are coloured in various bronze hues as a nod to the state's geology, giving the stadium a distinctly Western Australian feel. Inside, fans are well looked after: the circulation spaces still allow for views of the field so there's no reason to miss a moment of the action and, perhaps the most eagerly anticipated of the stadium's attributes, every seat is equipped with a cup holder, making beer spillage a thing of the past.

While the majority of stadiums and their surrounding areas lie dormant until game day, Perth Stadium was designed to activate its immediate surroundings, giving it purpose for 365 days a year. The landscaping is inspired by Indigenous creation stories and based around the six seasons according to the Noongar people. With a number of permanent artworks and plenty of spots to linger next to the Swan River, entertainment inside the stadium has a lot to contend with.

PERTH STADIUM

ARCHITECT
HASSELL, HKS and Cox Architecture

CLIENT
Government of Western Australia

YEAR OF COMPLETION
2017

COST
$1.6 billion

STYLE
Contemporary

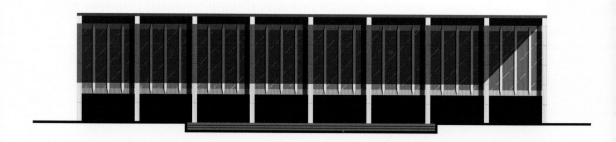

PERTH CONCERT HALL

5 ST GEORGES TERRACE, PERTH

ST GEORGES TERRACE

Originally designed in the form of a cylindrical auditorium as part of Jeffrey Howlett and Don Bailey's winning design for Council House, Perth Concert Hall was put off for several years due to financial constraints. The project was restarted in 1968 with a brief to build Australia's first concert hall following the second World War. The building was to occupy the site of the half-finished foundations of the unbuilt 23-storey Chevron-Hilton Hotel, the construction of which was abandoned when its financial backing collapsed. The original cylindrical design was abandoned in favour of the acutely rectangular and gridded structure of the Brutalist Concert Hall that opened some seven months before the Sydney Opera House.

The imposing Late Twentieth Century Stripped Classical facade is a superb example of Australian Brutalist public architecture. The foyer is truly a beauty to behold: white Japanese board-marked concrete cast with New Zealand Oregon timber moulds contrast gorgeously with the rich reds of the carpets and jarrah detailing. Monolithic concrete columns and beams all interlock and balance atop each other, leaving gaps where light streams through. Breaking the strict grid of rectangular geometry is a large concrete spiral staircase that winds itself around a gigantic concrete cylinder that houses the elevator. The hall has hosted acts as renowned as Ray Charles and the London Philharmonic, and events as humble as local school speech days and performances. It seats over 1,700 people and houses an organ of over 3,000 pipes. The Concert Hall received the coveted Enduring Architecture Award at the 2016 Australian Institute of Architects National Awards, placing it firmly on the map at a national scale; the jury commended the building for being '… hung from itself, creating enormous free spans and all from one beautifully poured material.'

PERTH CONCERT HALL

ARCHITECT
Howlett & Bailey Architects

CLIENT
Government of Western Australia and City of Perth

YEAR OF COMPLETION
1973

COST
$3.1 million

STYLE
Late Twentieth Century Stripped Classical / Brutalist

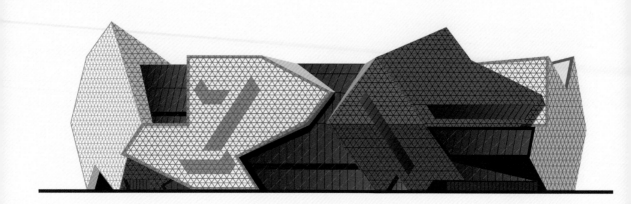

PERTH ARENA

700 WELLINGTON STREET, PERTH

Inspired by the twelve sides of Fremantle's Roundhouse and some of the 209 irregularly shaped pieces of Christopher Monckton's 1999 Eternity Puzzle, Perth Arena is truly an architectural statement like no other. Three parts Rubik's cube, one part spaceship, this superbly detailed Postmodern marvel has more to it than meets the eye. There are illusions, props, and visual magic tricks at play inside and out. Standing in just the right spot in front of the blue mishmash of steel that forms the entrance canopy reveals a forced perspective, perfectly framing the pieces of the arena puzzle.

The building has quickly become a cornerstone of the CBD in both a literal and symbolic sense. It was the first stage of the Perth City Link project that spans nearly a kilometre to Yagan Square and the Horseshoe Bridge, and involved the sinking of the Perth to Fremantle railway to connect the CBD with Northbridge.

Monckton's Eternity Puzzle was a tiling puzzle that was marketed as being unsolvable, a fact that toy company Ertl was so confident of that they offered a £1 million prize for anyone who could solve it within four years. It took just over a year for two mathematicians from Cambridge University to solve the puzzle and collect the prize money. Renowned for their alternative approach to architecture, ARM chose ten pieces of the Eternity Puzzle that resemble aspects of Perth life: a sail boat, a swan, a cockatoo, the shape of Rottnest Island and Western Australia, a drill rig and a haul truck. Each piece is arranged around the arena to form the facade, with the gaps between them filled by large spans of triangulated glazing that enclose the public concourses inside. As with the exterior, you will be hard-pressed to find a rectilinear space anywhere within the public areas of the interior.

The versatile arena has hosted Grammy Award–winning superstars including Elton John, Katy Perry and the Rolling Stones, as well as being the home of the Perth Wildcats National Basketball League team and the annual international Hopman Cup tennis tournament. It is a unique piece of abstract art, on a very grand scale, that has become part of the city's identity and will continue to be for many decades to come.

PERTH ARENA

ARCHITECT
ARM Architecture and Cameron Chisholm Nicol

CLIENT
Government of Western Australia

YEAR OF COMPLETION
2012

COST
$548.7 million

STYLE
Twenty-first Century Postmodernist/Deconstructivist

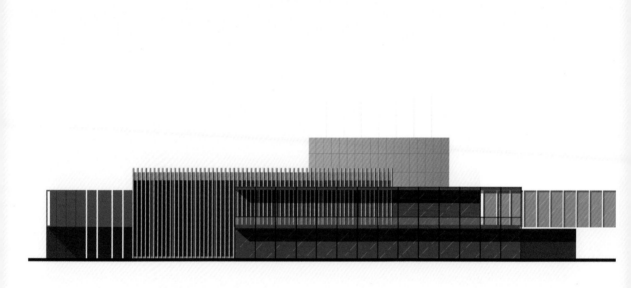

STATE THEATRE CENTRE
OF WESTERN AUSTRALIA

174–176 WILLIAM STREET, PERTH

The State Theatre Centre of Western Australia is a masterpiece of Contemporary civic architecture, the result of an international design competition in 2005, with Kerry Hill Architects' design chosen from over 40 entries.

The building comprises several rectilinear masses, each with its own distinct character and materiality that embody the recurring design concept of opposing forces. These masses gently intersect each other to form a whole that is even greater than the sum of its parts. These opposing forces perform a narrative that is as dramatic as the performances within: a soaring charcoal canopy draws you into a dazzling foyer laden with gold and warm timbers, leading to a great timber drum that houses the main theatre, named for the late Australian actor Heath Ledger. The efficient arrangement of vertically stacked theatres allows for a civic space in the form of a courtyard that weaves its way between original William Street shopfronts and the Cultural Centre behind – an ingenious response to the cramped conditions that inevitably accompany an inner-city site. The basement-level Studio Underground black box theatre and the courtyard with space for 200 seats make up the alternative performance spaces.

Public art has been integrated into the site as part of the state government's Percent for Art public art scheme, with two artworks that respond to the building and the history of the site. *Falling from Heaven to Earth; The Shooting Star* by Matthew Ngui is a spectacular interactive public art piece that lies across the floor of the Roe Street entrance. A display of lights is triggered by the movement of people through the space, projecting patterns of heat and cold, fire and ice on the glass floor, representative of a shooting star falling to Earth. *Interval*, a sound installation and series of stainless steel panels with text and imagery at the James Street entrance, forms the second public artwork by artists Arif Satar, Audrey Fernandes Satar and Sam Landels. A continuous recording of voices emanates from within the wall, telling oral histories of the site in a poetic manner.

STATE THEATRE CENTRE OF WESTERN AUSTRALIA

ARCHITECT
Kerry Hill Architects

CLIENT
Government of Western Australia

YEAR OF COMPLETION
2011

COST
$91 million

STYLE
Contemporary / Twenty-first Century Postmodernist

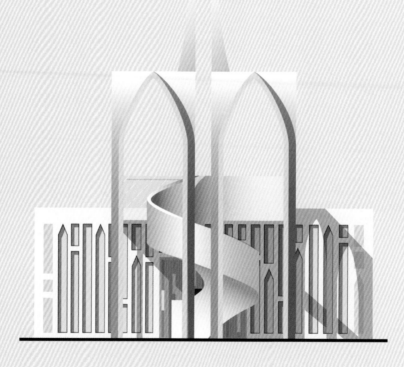

CADOGAN SONG SCHOOL

38 ST GEORGES TERRACE, PERTH

ST GEORGES TERRACE

Sandwiched between the towering St George's Cathedral, the historic Burt Memorial Hall and the Deanery lies a curious little building called the Cadogan Song School. The building itself is a collage of sorts, taking forms from its neighbours and other features of cathedral architecture and abstracting, contemporising and combining them. The end product of this assembly of borrowed elements is a building with a unique identity: all of the forms work in harmony to deliver something beautiful.

Generously funded by the eighth Earl Cadogan, a wealthy British aristocrat, the Song School was designed primarily to house the St George's Cathedral choirs while preserving sightlines and creating more cohesive pathways through the site and between the Cathedral and Burt Memorial Hall. It consists of a rehearsal and recording hall that has been designed to match the acoustics of the Cathedral, enswathed with white American oak from the parquetry to the bespoke furniture, as well as a library to house an extensive music collection. The vaulted ceiling of the hall, consisting of softly curving concrete beams bordering perforated brass panels, is a nod to the classical underground crypts often found in the depths of cathedrals.

Externally, the iconic dual rows of crisp white vaulted archways, 'tuning fork' spire and the spiral staircase, stunningly detailed in its design, are of an international standard, and have hosted many a photo opportunity. The precast concrete modular vaults were manufactured by specialists in Adelaide in order to meet the high standard of finish required, before being trucked across the Nullarbor. They are positioned very slightly splayed apart from each other in the shape of an X. This imperceptible detail creates a forced perspective that allows the viewer to discern all rows of archways from all angles: an example of the extraordinary level of thought that has gone into the design. It may seem an odd turn of phrase to use in this particular instance, but the devil is truly in the details.

CADOGAN SONG SCHOOL

ARCHITECT
Palassis Architects

CLIENT
Perth Diocesan Trustees

YEAR OF COMPLETION
2017

COST
$4.9 million

STYLE
Contemporary / Twenty-first Century Postmodernist

ST GEORGE'S CATHEDRAL

38 ST GEORGES TERRACE, PERTH

ST GEORGES TERRACE

Located just off the terrace that bears the same name, St George's Cathedral sits on sacred ground: near the location of the jarrah tree under which the first Anglican service in the Swan River Colony was held in 1829. A square of timber from this very tree is housed near the brass lectern from the original Church of St George of 1845, which was the one of the first churches in Western Australia, serving a population of less than 4,000 people when it was built. When the burgeoning population outgrew the original church, it was demolished and, over the space of a decade, was replaced with the current cathedral, completed in 1888. Many of the furnishings of the original church were retained and relocated to the new cathedral, including the organ, which was manufactured by the same firm that rebuilt Westminster Abbey's organ in 1884. The iconic square bell tower was built at a cost of £1,129 in 1902 as a memorial to Queen Victoria, who had passed away one year prior. The tower was designed by Sir J.J. Talbot Hobbs in the Victorian Tudor style, and is noticeably similar to the tower at St George's College with its crenelated parapet and tourelle – also designed by Hobbs for the Anglican Church.

St George's is one of very few cathedrals in the world made primarily from handmade bricks, all of which came from brickyards along the Swan River. Limestone for the windows and quoins was quarried at Rottnest Island, and the impressive jarrah hammerbeam trusses in the ceiling had to be laid in the Swan River for two years to become soft enough for bending and carving. Walking into the cathedral is truly awe-inspiring: the vastness of the space and quality of finishes and detailing is something that's often a rarity in a city less than 200 years old.

ARCHITECT
Edmund Thomas Blacket

CLIENT
Anglican Diocese of Perth

YEAR OF COMPLETION
1888

COST
£17,000

STYLE
Victorian Academic Gothic

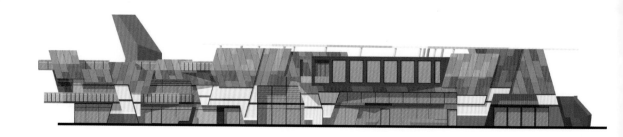

YAGAN SQUARE

WELLINGTON STREET, PERTH

Since the late 1800s, Perth's central business district has been severed from Northbridge by the railway, with few crossing points near the city. In a bid to reunite the CBD with its northern neighbours, the long-overdue Perth City Link project was established. Its crowning centerpiece is Yagan Square, a civic space complete with play areas, a market hall, performance venues and retail tenancies.

The square is named after Yagan, a Noongar warrior who became notorious for his bravery in resisting European settlement of the Swan River – a statue of Yagan stands proudly on Heirisson Island east of the city. The precinct is a beautifully considered civic hub, taking inspiration from the history of the ground on which it sits and designed in conjunction with the traditional owners of the land. The concept is based largely around the idea of convergence, with references made to the ancient tracks which used to crisscross the region, leading people to their meeting places, as the tracks through the square continue to do today.

The building's form and materiality reflect the unique geology of the state: locally sourced timber, granite and limestone give a feel for the diverse colours and textures found across Western Australia. The shimmering silver shade canopies are symbolic of the lakes and rivers which once flowed through the site, while the protruding columns above the cylindrical digital screen signify the bulrushes that grew beside them. Public artwork features heavily throughout the precinct, including *Waterline* by Jon Tarry, which features water that bubbles up from the 'source' in the children's play area, making its way down past the amphitheatre to ground level to meet the nine-metre sculpture called *Wirin* – the Noongar word for spirit – by Tjyllyungoo / Lance Chad. Yagan Square successfully delivers some vital connections: from Northbridge to the city, the city to its history and the people to each other.

YAGAN SQUARE

ARCHITECT
Lyons Architecture and Iredale Pedersen Hook with landscape architects ASPECT Studios

CLIENT
Government of Western Australia

YEAR OF COMPLETION
2018

COST
$73.5 million

STYLE
Twenty-first Century Postmodernist

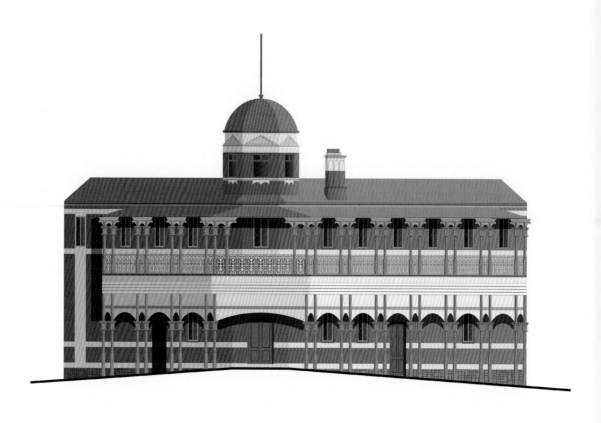

ROYAL GEORGE HOTEL

34 DUKE STREET, EAST FREMANTLE

DUKE STREET

ROYAL GEORGE HOTEL

The pub that moved a highway and lived to tell the tale, the Royal George Hotel is a fine example of a gold rush era hotel, showing all the flare and confidence of a city in boom time. Built for prominent West Australian publicans and successful prospectors the Mulcahy brothers, it served its original purpose quenching the thirsts of East Fremantle locals and providing lodging until 1980, when it was acquired by Main Roads Western Australia. Not traditionally known for their drinking establishments, Main Roads had planned to bulldoze the historic hotel in favour of the Stirling Highway extension, to the despair of locals and those with an affinity for the old pub. Thanks to protests held in North Fremantle, David beat Goliath and the highway was moved (slightly), but the George would endure a relatively quiet next 40 years. It was used briefly as a school, then as an art and community centre before it was acquired by the National Trust. The trust oversaw many proposals for restoration while it sat empty, but most fell through due to the prohibitive cost of renewal. The building had grown increasingly derelict and just when it looked like all hope was lost, plans to restore and develop the site were announced with the design in the safe hands of spaceagency: architects. Their design for the multimillion dollar development sees the hotel restored to its former glory and adjoined by a number of high quality residential apartments, while activating the surrounding public spaces.

ARCHITECT
Emil Mauermann

CLIENT
Daniel and Michael Mulcahy

YEAR OF COMPLETION
1903

COST
£5,200

STYLE
Federation Free Classical

INDIANA COTTESLOE

99 MARINE PARADE, COTTESLOE

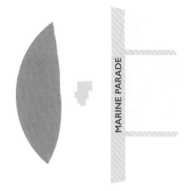

Few buildings on this list can claim to have achieved the icon status that Indiana has in such a relatively short space of time. It has become a symbol of Perth's idyllic beachy west-coast lifestyle and has fronted many a postcard and tourism campaign.

Indiana sits perched on a hill above Cottesloe, Perth's oldest and most treasured recreational beach, managing to look as if it has done so for a century. The result of a submission to the council by Laurie Scanlan of Scanlan Architects in 1994, the building was inspired in part by its predecessor, the Centenary Bathing Pavilion, which was the winning entry in a design competition by Oswald Chisholm, an early partner of renowned local firm Cameron Chisholm Nicol. The design combines elements of the Late Twentieth Century Postmodern and Australian Nostalgic architectural styles, with arch windows that will take you back to the days of *Play School*, and grand interiors that reflect a bygone era.

The eponymous Indiana Tea House was built in 1910 to serve the countless modestly dressed swimmers that frequented the heavily populated stretch of beach. This was replaced by the Centenary Bathing Pavilion in 1929, which stood for just over 50 years before structural issues resulted in its demolition in 1982. Its replacement the following year was a much simpler Postmodern (and very 80s) affair. It wasn't long before calls were made for the upgrade that the area sorely needed. Scanlan's proposal maintained portions of the 1980s pavilion, opting to build over and around it. The design was intended to appear as if it had been there for 40 or 50 years, and it does so fairly successfully, though it is worth noting that this is an act that is almost universally discouraged since the advent of Modernist architecture. It was a gamble that paid off, as the building has become the most recognisable on the endless West Australian coastline.

INDIANA COTTESLOE

ARCHITECT
Scanlan Architects

CLIENT
Town of Cottesloe

YEAR OF COMPLETION
1996

COST
Unknown

STYLE
Late Twentieth Century Postmodern / Australian Nostalgic

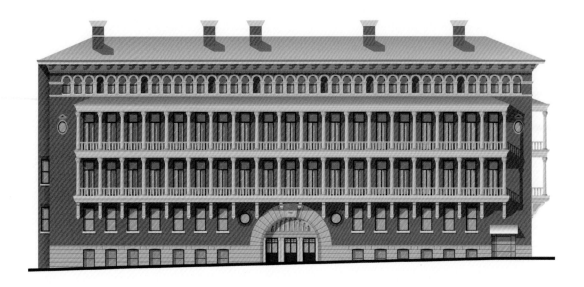

FORMER TITLES OFFICE

CATHEDRAL AVENUE, PERTH

CATHEDRAL AVENUE

FORMER TITLES OFFICE

With more French doors and Corinthian columns than you can poke a stick at, George Temple Poole's final addition to the venerated Cathedral Square precinct is a masterpiece that has been long admired by locals since its completion in 1897. The former Titles Office was designed in the Italian Renaissance tradition and sits opposite the Victorian Academic Gothic St George's Cathedral and beside the Victorian Second Empire–styled Treasury buildings, consolidating the city's most architecturally diverse precinct. Poole was renowned for designing buildings that were sympathetic to their surroundings without directly mimicking them. His architectural good manners can be observed in the building's colonnades that echo that above the western entrance of the cathedral opposite – one of many small gestures that make the precinct feel as one whole, despite the plethora of different styles.

The Titles building was extensively renovated along with the rest of the State Buildings in a mammoth eight-year rejuvenation of the precinct involving Kerry Hill Architects and Palassis Architects that included the new City of Perth Library and concluded in 2017. The precinct won an impressive number of awards, including George Temple Poole awards for both the State Buildings and for the City of Perth Library and Public Plaza, the first time in the award's history that the highest honour in Western Australian architecture has been shared. The Titles building now houses part of the COMO The Treasury hotel, which has been awarded the best hotel in Australia and New Zealand three times by *Condé Nast Traveller*.

ARCHITECT
George Temple Poole

CLIENT
Government of Western Australia

YEAR OF COMPLETION
1897

COST
£21,200

STYLE
Federation Free Classical

OLD TREASURY BUILDINGS

CORNER BARRACK STREET AND ST GEORGES TERRACE

The year 1870 saw an increase in Perth's public works program, partially due to Western Australia being granted representative government and a resulting ability to raise loans. However, when the first step was taken to create what is now arguably the city's most significant heritage precinct, it was a somewhat cautious one. Richard Roach Jewell's first offering to the selected site for the new government offices was a well-proportioned, modest two-storey building fronting Barrack Street. Despite the attractive varying hues of the buildings' Flemish bond brickwork, the public was not impressed with this architectural style, with the West Australian describing this type of building as 'a rectangular brick box with a few holes in it for doors and windows'. It was clear that the fledgling government would require something more elaborate to impress the people of Perth.

George Temple Poole's design for the General Post Office was realised in 1890, linking together Jewell's existing eastern and western wings. In a show of architectural good manners, Poole retained the proportions and materiality of the former works but added an air of elegance with Classical ornamentation around the windows and doors. He later added a third storey topped with a high mansard roof reminiscent of a Parisian mansion. In the early 1900s, Jewell's original buildings underwent a facelift at the hands of John Harry Grainger, bringing them in line with Poole's GPO. The openings were adorned with the same ornamentation, and a third storey with a similar roof form was constructed.

During the second half of the twentieth century, there was a steady exodus of the various government departments from the precinct, the last leaving in 1993. The buildings sat empty for nearly 20 years before the work of Kerry Hill Architects and Palassis Architects gave them a new lease on life. The $90 million project transformed the buildings into a vibrant hospitality and retail destination, home to a luxury 48-suite hotel and some of Perth's finest bars and eateries. Fittingly the work was commended with Western Australia's most prestigious architectural accolade – the George Temple Poole Award.

ST GEORGES TERRACE

OLD TREASURY BUILDINGS

ARCHITECT
Richard Roach Jewell (Public Offices); George Temple Poole (GPO and extensions)

CLIENT
Government of Western Australia

YEAR OF COMPLETION
1874 (Public Offices); 1882 (Treasury); 1890 (GPO)

COST
£3,900 (eastern wing only); £9,500 (GPO)

STYLE
Victorian Second Empire

QVI

250 ST GEORGES TERRACE, PERTH

ST GEORGES TERRACE

QV1

With a name curiously derived from the Latin phrase 'quo vadis', meaning 'whither goest thou?', QV1 is one of the few entries in this book that is nearly as beautiful in plan as it is in reality. Undoubtedly one of the finest skyscrapers of the Perth skyline, this diamond in the rough was criticised by some upon its completion as Perth's most ugly building. QV1 was designed by one of Australia's most treasured Modernist architects, Harry Seidler, who considered it to be one of his finest buildings.

The intent behind the design of the 42-storey tower was that it would not be yet another monument to commerce, but instead would cater for the wellbeing of its users . This humanistic approach to designing office buildings has since become the norm but, when completed, the large open public spaces and garden terraces scattered across the facade of QV1 certainly set it apart from other office spaces in Perth's CBD.

At the tower's base, two imposing stone-clad curved legs frame the grand entrance off St Georges Terrace, both sheltered under a great Marilyn Monroe-esque floating glass 'skirt'. Internally the imposing fourteen-metre-high lobby dotted with polished granite columns elicits the desired effect of making you wish you'd donned your shiniest shoes that morning. Overall, the building adopts what can only be described as a 'mullet' methodology: strong and precise geometric gestures (business) in the front; free-flowing curves forming the retail and public space (party) in the back.

ARCHITECT
Harry Seidler & Associates

CLIENT
Barrack Properties, Kajima Corporation and Interstruct

YEAR OF COMPLETION
1991

COST
$340 million

STYLE
Late Twentieth Century Modernist

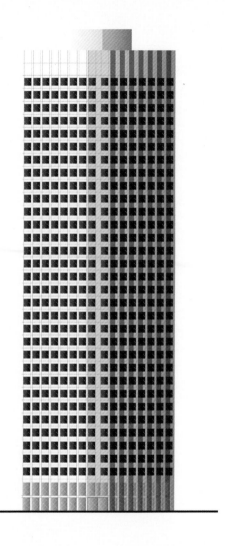

ALLENDALE SQUARE

77 ST GEORGES TERRACE, PERTH

ALLENDALE SQUARE

This great anodised aluminium-clad tower was the tallest building on the Perth skyline upon its completion in the midst of a minerals boom, topping out at a height of 132 metres. Its rise above the rest was thanks to the cunning 45-degree rotation off St Georges Terrace, increasing the facade-to-curb distance and therefore allowing extra storeys under the city council's rules.

When built, Allendale Square was a symbol of the city's prosperity and set a precedent for skyscrapers to come. Through clever planning and meticulous design, the building performs incredibly well environmentally. The diamond orientation and stepped sawtooth facade result in windows that are exclusively north-south oriented, while only solid panels face east and west, limiting direct sun exposure. Views out from the offices over the Swan River can be enjoyed without interruption due to the columnless design, with floors spanning from central lift core to facade without additional vertical supports.

At the base of the tower is a spacious forecourt to St Georges Terrace that emphasises the public aspect and precise drama of the facade above. The building's other features include a pedestrian plaza, an underground shopping concourse and a Brutalist chapel. A recent renovation by Christou Design Group saw the rejuvenation of the underground and ground levels, as well as the addition of an elegant floating glass canopy.

ARCHITECT
Cameron, Chisholm & Nicol

CLIENT
Unkown

YEAR OF COMPLETION
1976

COST
Unknown

STYLE
Late Twentieth Century Modernist

AUSTRALIAN INSTITUTE OF ARCHITECTS

33

FORMER DAVID FOULKES TAYLOR SHOWROOM

33 BROADWAY, NEDLANDS

Now the home of architecture in Western Australia, the former David Foulkes Taylor Showroom in Nedlands has always been a hub of design talent. The very modest building was commissioned by the highly regarded furniture maker David Foulkes Taylor to display his range of bespoke furniture, as well as imported modern furniture and homewares. The up-and-coming Perth architect Julius Elischer designed the showroom to echo the works of revolutionary Modernist architects Adolf Loos and Le Corbusier. Elischer himself was born in pre–World War II Europe at a time when the Bauhaus movement was in full swing.

The white painted brick walls of the showroom support a number of suspended steel platforms which break up the vast cubic volume with multiple mezzanine floors. The iconic small segmented windows with deep reveals create a unique dappled light inside, a device used by Elischer to ensure direct sunlight would not cause any of the upholsteries on display to fade. The reveals were originally painted in rich, earthy colours, though the current primary colour scheme adds to the unique light and colour of the interior experience as well as creating a more approachable facade to contrast the stark white mass. A tropical-inspired garden by landscape architect Paul Robinson softens what would otherwise be a rather jarring rectilinear box.

The showroom as it stands was only intended as stage one of a two-stage development. The objective was to include an alfresco cafe and restaurant as a 'total lifestyle concept' – an idea that, though commonplace today, would have been rather novel at the time. Unfortunately, this proposal remained forever unrealised due to David Foulkes Taylor's untimely death in a car accident in 1966.

FORMER DAVID FOULKES TAYLOR SHOWROOM

ARCHITECT
Julius Elischer

CLIENT
David Foulkes Taylor

YEAR OF COMPLETION
1965

COST
Unknown

STYLE
Late Twentieth Century Brutalist

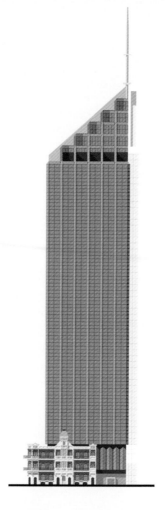

PALACE HOTEL AND
108 ST GEORGES TERRACE

108 ST GEORGES TERRACE, PERTH

From one of Perth's earliest taverns to a 214-metre skyscraper, the corner of St Georges Terrace and William Street has seen some dramatic architectural change over the years. The King's Head Hotel, Perth's first licensed venue, was erected on the site in around 1830 and sold shortly after to early settler William Leeder, the man from whom Leederville takes its name. Western Australia's first masonic lodge was later added to the pub, which after Leeder's death was run by his wife until the 1880s. American real estate investor John De Baun purchased the building in 1894 and ran an architectural competition to design a new hotel for the site. The flamboyant winning entry came from architects Porter and Thomas, the building becoming their first commission in Perth.

On its completion, praise for the Palace Hotel was universal. Externally, the handsome Romanesque facade, intricate balustrades and dramatic entryway topped with a 26-metre tower made for a stately welcome. Internally, the hotel's amenities placed its visitors in the lap of luxury. An electric lift saved patrons' legs from the tiresome stairs of its three storeys and all 216 rooms were equipped with electric lighting, including the bathrooms and corridors.

While it's hard to imagine the city centre without the iconic hotel, its future was at risk when it was bought by the Commonwealth Bank in the 1970s with plans to replace it with offices – a fate met by many high-quality heritage buildings during this era. A reprieve was granted to the hotel by a group of outraged members of the public who went by the moniker 'Palace Guards'. Not only did they save the Palace, they saw it given a protected future in the form of a heritage listing. After the Commonwealth Bank's plan for the building fell apart, it was purchased by famed Perth businessman Alan Bond. Architects Cameron, Chisholm & Nicol designed the 52-storey Bankwest (formerly R&I Bank) Tower to sit over the top of the old hotel, becoming Perth's tallest piece of architecture upon completion. The skyscraper's triangular shape aims its visual focus towards the views over the Swan River, which Bond was able to admire from his penthouse apartment housing his US$54 million purchase of van Gogh's *Irises*. The form lends itself to open-plan office space and allows in natural light, with a saw-toothed facade creating multiple corner offices from which to admire the view.

ST GEORGES TERRACE

PALACE HOTEL AND 108 ST GEORGES TERRACE

ARCHITECT
Ernest Saunders Porter and Edmond Neville Thomas (Palace Hotel); Cameron, Chisholm & Nicol (former Bankwest Tower)

CLIENT
John De Baun; Alan Bond

YEAR OF COMPLETION
1897; 1989

COST
£64,000; $120 million

STYLE
Federation Free Classical; Late Twentieth Century Postmodernist

LONDON COURT

647 HAY STREET, PERTH

If ever the multitude of Perth's British expats feel a pang of longing for the comforts of Blighty, refuge can always be sought in the city's little slice of London. The arcade connecting Hay Street with St Georges Terrace was designed to perfectly reflect the Tudor style of fifteenth century London. The building features steeply gabled roofs topped with weathercocks, gargoyles, masks, shields and crests adorning all available surfaces, and half-timbered walling on the facades. Inside the arcade, visitors are watched over by the statues of two quintessentially British figures – Dick Whittington and Sir Walter Raleigh. Perhaps the most well-known features of London Court are the clocks which hang on the external facades at each end of the arcade. The dial at the St Georges Terrace end is a copy of the Great Clock at Rouen in France, while the one facing Hay Street is a replica of one of the world's most famous time pieces – Big Ben.

The inspiration for the building came from Edwin Thomas Hall's design of the Liberty department store in London, another mock-Tudor construction completed in 1924. Both designs came under criticism from the architecture community for being imitative and not in the 'modern' style of the time. However, beneath its 'olde' English skin, London Court remained very much up to date with building techniques of the day. The structure was built predominantly of steel and concrete, with electric elevators servicing the flats and office spaces over the ground floor tenancies. The 24 flats on the upper floors, which have since given way to office space, were fitted out with electrical appliances, including the first air-conditioning system in Western Australia to allow both heating and cooling.

Initially built by the notoriously shady goldminer and financier Claude de Bernales, London Court was sold to London Court Pty Ltd, its current owners, around 1952 following the collapse of de Bernales's companies after a police investigation into alleged embezzlement. To this day, the arcade continues to be a popular tourist attraction and shopping destination in Perth's centre. Every fifteen minutes, the two clocks entertain the crowds with their shows, in which tournament knights circle on Hay Street, while at the south end, St George does battle with a dragon.

LONDON COURT

ARCHITECT
Bernard Evans and Oldham, Boas & Ednie-Brown

CLIENT
Claude de Bernales

YEAR OF COMPLETION
1937

COST
£100,000

STYLE
Inter-war Old English

GLEDDEN BUILDING

731 HAY STREET

The only high-rise Inter-war Art Deco office building in Perth, the Gledden Building's design was described by the *Sunday Times* upon its completion in 1938 as 'the modernistic vertical type of gothic architecture', a style that had become synonymous with thriving modern cities like New York and Los Angeles. The building was named after Robert John Gledden, one of the pioneering surveyors of the Coolgardie goldfields. He bequeathed his entire estate, including the land on which the building sits, to the University of Western Australia upon his death in 1927. His will nobly stated that the net income from the estate should go towards the promotion and encouragement of education, particularly that relating to surveying, engineering and mining. Designed by local legend Harold Boas of Oldham, Boas & Ednie-Brown as a symbol of Perth's post-Depression optimism, the building is a sterling example of Art Deco ideals, fusing decorative art and architecture. To say the building was state-of-the-art for the time would be an understatement. The extent of the integration of electricity, lighting, lifts and other services was unprecedented, and even included an 'electric clock service' that supplied each of the eight floors with the correct time.

A competition was announced in 1937 by the Vice-Chancellor of UWA for the design of a 46-metre frieze along the internal arcade. The competition declared the frieze could contain figures of the 'men, trees or beasts' of Western Australia, with a budget of £250 for the construction and £21 for first prize. The winning artwork by George Benson displays a mix of Western Australian themes including Aborigines and their environment, mythical and cultural beliefs – a highly progressive subject matter for the time. The emphasis and appreciation of the civic value of public art begun by this competition marked something of a turning point, albeit one that wasn't observed for many years afterwards, due to the emergence of World War II the year after the building's completion. The war effort also put a hold on aspirational architecture like that of the Gledden building – another high-rise office building wasn't constructed in Perth until 1954.

HAY STREET

GLEDDEN BUILDING

ARCHITECT
Oldham, Boas & Ednie-Brown

CLIENT
University of Western Australia

YEAR OF COMPLETION
1938

COST
£36,800

STYLE
Inter-war Art Deco

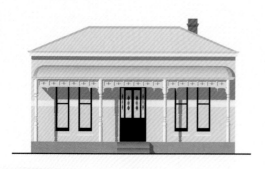

VICTORIAN WORKERS' COTTAGE

1840–1901

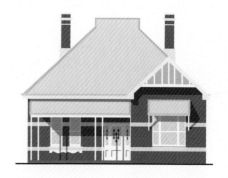

FEDERATION BUNGALOW

1890–1915

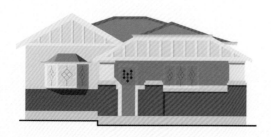

CALIFORNIA BUNGALOW

1915–1940

ART DECO

1930–1960

POST-WAR

1945–1965

INTERNATIONAL

1940–1960

IMMIGRANTS' NOSTALGIC

1915–1940

McMANSION

1985–2020

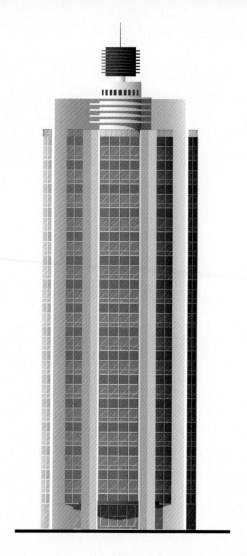

MOUNT ELIZA APARTMENTS

71 MOUNT STREET, WEST PERTH

On the banks of Mount Eliza, there is a curious rocket-like building lovingly known to many in Perth as 'the Thermos'. The cylindrical apartment building arose out of the same mid-century futurist utopian thinking that gave the world the Jetsons and Disney's Tomorrowland. The building was the second tallest in Perth when it was completed in 1964, though its position on the hill made it tower above anything else in the area, as it continues to do over 50 years later. The building's location is also the reason behind the enormous water tower crown, necessary due to its elevation high above the nearby Mount Eliza reservoir.

The Mount Eliza Apartments were designed by local multi-residential legends Krantz & Sheldon, who were responsible for an astonishing amount of Perth's high-quality walk-up flats and high-rise apartments from the 1930s to the 1980s. The tower marks the change in generation from Harold Krantz to his son David, who assisted his father in designing the slightly more modest low-rise apartments that preceded it. The building was received as rather controversial at the time, considered to be a Modernist intrusion on an otherwise uninterrupted natural landscape. The building's structure, circulation and use of space planning are incredibly well-designed and efficient even for today's standards. Vertical circulation is achieved via two interlocking circular stairways that form a double helix around the two lifts. The top five storeys offer one apartment per floor, each with an unrivalled 360-degree view of Perth, from the hills to the ocean, with each floor below containing two semi-circular apartments. The design is extraordinarily unique in that the dual helical staircases and lifts mean the floors with two apartments do not share a corridor or a lift, while each of the top five apartments have access from two separate entrances via two stairways and lifts.

MOUNT ELIZA APARTMENTS

ARCHITECT
Krantz & Sheldon

CLIENT
Unknown

YEAR OF COMPLETION
1964

COST
Unknown

STYLE
Late Twentieth Century Modernist

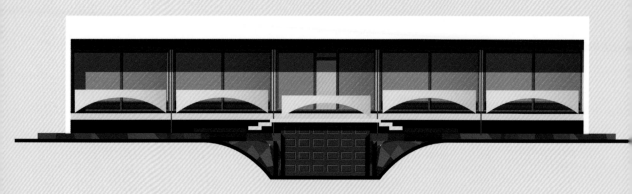

PAGANIN HOUSE

165 THE BOULEVARD, FLOREAT

THE BOULEVARD

PAGANIN HOUSE

Iwan Iwanoff's houses have earned a cult status among Perth's architecture admirers – the Bulgarian-born, German-trained architect is a local legend. Built for the Paganin family, this house is an excellent example of the international style, taking cues from the Case Study Houses of Los Angeles and Mies van der Rohe's revered Barcelona Pavilion, with hints of Iwanoff's signature expressionist style. It demonstrates a mastery of visual balance and composition that will stop you in your tracks. Complete with a sunken lounge, three bars, a ten-metre swimming pool, sauna, golf course frontage and laden with bespoke furniture and details, the house yearns to entertain.

While open-plan living has become commonplace in modern housing, Iwanoff was something of a pioneer of the style in Western Australia. Paganin House is no exception. The abundant light and lack of dividing walls is complemented by the extensive use of marble and timber, which make up much of the internal material palette.

Tragically, in 2015 Paganin House was destroyed by fire, which led to an outpouring of grief from those who had admired it for the last 50 years. As a testament to its importance and significance to the owners and community, it has been painstakingly rebuilt, and will no doubt inspire another 50 years worth of passers-by.

ARCHITECT
Iwan Iwanoff

CLIENT
Private resident

YEAR OF COMPLETION
1965

COST
Unknown

STYLE
Post-war International/
Modernist

32 HENRY STREET APARTMENTS

32 HENRY STREET, FREMANTLE

HENRY STREET

32 HENRY STREET APARTMENTS

Although now over a decade old, the spaceagency-designed Henry Street apartments somehow manage to look as if they were built yesterday. The stripped-back, contemporary floating block of ten units sits above and behind the partial ruins of an old Victorian workers' cottage in Fremantle's historic West End. Henry Street has been around as long as the city itself, with its first licensed public house popping up as early as 1833, and many of its heritage-listed buildings remain. At number 32, the Flemish bond brick facade, limestone side wall and dilapidated timber verandah were all that remained before the development in 2009.

The asymmetry of the hefty front column makes it appear to support the entirety of the apartments above from one side, while the other side of the building hovers cantilevered above the former cottage below,

separated by a 30-centimetre gap of frameless glazing. This slight separation reinforces the idea that the two are indeed two separate entities that share a synergistic, rather than antithetic relationship.

When looking south from High Street, the cantilevered white box peeks out from behind the collage of Victorian and Federation architecture that the West End is known for, managing to look perfectly at home despite its comparative simplicity. In the architect's own words, the concept was to integrate contemporary architecture into the heritage environment in a way that 'expresses continuity between the past, present and future.' By picking up some of the horizontal lines of its High Street neighbour, the building makes a stark contrast, but a welcome one; the two are of the same family, just a century apart.

ARCHITECT
spaceagency: architects
CLIENT
Unknown
YEAR OF COMPLETION
2009
COST
Unknown
STYLE
Twenty-first Century
International / Victorian
Georgian (original building)

WARDERS' COTTAGES

7–41 HENDERSON STREET, FREMANTLE

When the *Scindian* docked in Fremantle in 1850, bringing with it the first batch of convicts to the Swan River Colony, its unexpected arrival left the colony entirely unprepared. While a message had been sent from England, warning of the impending newcomers, it reached Western Australian after the convict ship had landed. The first stones for the Fremantle Prison would not be laid for another two years, during which time the original 75 convicts were housed in a woolshed and surrounding properties leased from the harbourmaster. As the young colony was set for a steady influx of British arrivals over the coming years, the immediate concern was accommodation for the warders and their families.

The need for the new buildings was so great that Captain Henderson, Comptroller-General of Convicts, chose to begin building work before receiving the go-ahead from London, eventually receiving approval for the cottages on the basis that they would be 'no frills' dwellings. The houses stand as a reminder of Western Australia's history of convict labour, and their present-day condition is a testament to how well they were built

by Henderson, with the assistance of Royal Engineer Lieutenant Henry Wray commanding the Twentieth Company of Engineers.

Of the three blocks of cottages built, one of the earliest examples of public housing in the state, the majority are still standing. The design was based on the workers' cottages in England, employing locally sourced materials for the solid limestone walls and shingled roofs. Updates and changes were made to the buildings over the years, including the addition of plumbing and external toilets coinciding with the arrival of mains sewerage to the town, but after the closure of Fremantle Prison in 1991, the cottages fell into a gradual state of decline. In 2011, they were declared unfit for inhabitants by the Department of Housing and their future looked bleak, but fortunes changed when ownership was assumed by the Western Australian Heritage Council. Since then, the buildings have undergone a $3 million restoration, allowing them to stand proudly once more as symbols of Fremantle's history. Today the cottages are inhabited again, and they have become prime real estate in the heart of the city.

WARDERS' COTTAGES

ARCHITECT
Edmund Yeamans Walcott Henderson and James Manning

CLIENT
British War and Colonial Office

YEAR OF COMPLETION
1858

COST
£4,300

STYLE
Victorian Georgian

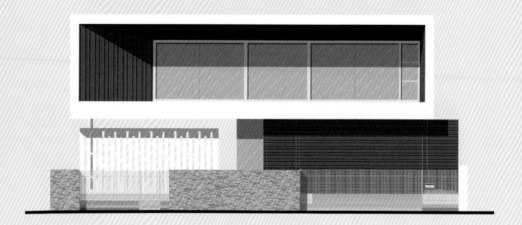

VICTORIA AVENUE HOUSE

101 VICTORIA AVENUE, DALKEITH

VICTORIA AVENUE

VICTORIA AVENUE HOUSE

The winner of the Marshall Clifton Award for Residential Architecture in 2016, Victoria Avenue house was designed by spaceagency, who are well known in Perth and Fremantle as designers of high-quality hospitality and residential projects, from the award-winning Petition at the State Buildings to Alex Hotel in Northbridge.

With a design that would fit right in amongst the iconic Modernist Case Study Houses of Los Angeles, this house in Dalkeith is the epitome of style. The two rectilinear forms that make up the building are stacked to create an L shape, with the lower level extending back into the block alongside a north-facing garden and swimming pool. This arrangement allows the entirety of the open-plan ground-floor, which includes the kitchen, living and dining rooms, to face the outdoors, while the upper level bedrooms have unobstructed views west to the river and east over the ground floor to the leafy suburbs beyond. By elevating the ground floor above the garden area, light is allowed into the basement garage via windows underneath a concrete verandah that steps down to the swimming pool, while a white concrete brise-soleil encloses the covered outdoor living area, draping strands of sunlight across it at sunset.

The restrained material palette of white concrete, timber and glass is contrasted beautifully by the heavily textured rammed concrete walls that form the plinth and entry wall. Every detail in this building has been carefully scrutinised, from the magnificent floating timber staircase and white concrete stairs below it that extend through low-level glazing to the exterior, to the edge-glazed vertical slots that penetrate the rammed concrete walls.

ARCHITECT
spaceagency: architects

CLIENT
Private resident

YEAR OF COMPLETION
2015

COST
Unknown

STYLE
Twenty-first Century International/Modernist

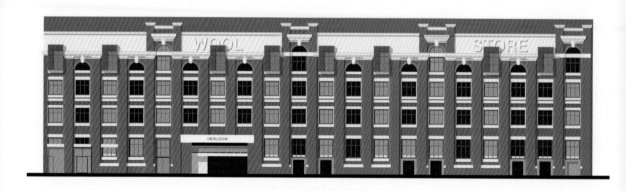

HEIRLOOM BY MATCH

36 QUEEN VICTORIA STREET, FREMANTLE

QUEEN VICTORIA STREET

Originally constructed for agriculture company Dalgety & Co., the vast brick warehouse overlooking the port of Fremantle is a wonderful reminder of the strength of Western Australia's wool industry. Although standing in a precinct once abounding with woolstores, when first built, Dalgety's was the largest in the state. Undoubtedly its size, along with its imposing facades and proximity to the centre of Fremantle, is what gave it a place close to the heart of many older locals. The original building, designed by Hobbs, Smith & Forbes, was only three floors. The architects had the foresight to ready the warehouse for expansion and in 1944 a fourth floor was added, along with the iconic sawtoothed roof structure visible above the eastern facade on the Queen Victoria Street side. When the store closed in the mid-1980s, it served briefly as a self-storage facility before being left abandoned for the best part of 20 years.

The question of how to respectfully adapt such a grand old heritage building into contemporary living was answered beautifully by the $70 million development of the woolstores in 2015. Architects Cameron Chisholm Nicol artfully slotted 183 apartments into the existing building, while largely maintaining and celebrating the original structure. The new work actively avoids any attempt to blend in with the old, delicately tiptoeing around it instead. The interior walls are offset from the retained jarrah columns and stop short of the ceilings to allow greater visibility of the original timber beams. Due to the extraordinary depth of the structure, natural light is delivered to all apartments by way of two atriums running the length of the building. These voids slice through the existing floors and roof form, dotted with protruding box-shaped balconies that reference the adjacent port and its numerous shipping containers. The original window openings have been retained on both facades and the iconic 'Wool Store' signage has been restored to its former glory. The building is a superb example of adaptive reuse without compromising heritage significance or quality of living.

HEIRLOOM BY MATCH

ARCHITECT
Hobbs, Smith & Forbes (woolstore); Cameron Chisholm Nicol (redevelopment)

CLIENT
Dalgety & Co.; Match

YEAR OF COMPLETION
1923; 2016

COST
£75,000; $70 million

STYLE
Federation Warehouse; Twenty-first Century Postmodernist

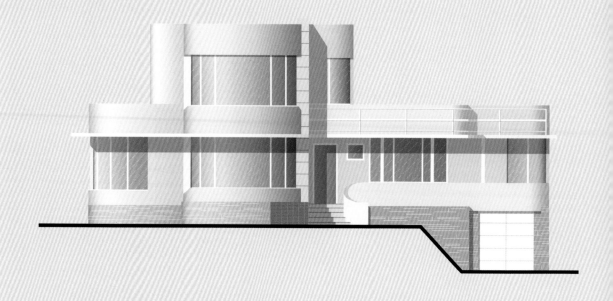

BLUE WATERS

CANNING HIGHWAY

Perth's Art Deco party palace, formerly a home of glitz and glamor in Western Australia, still conjures up images of the 1950s socialite lifestyle. Mabel and Keith Perron (brother to Perth billionaire Stan Perron, whose Central Park skyscraper can be seen from the first-floor windows) based the design on a 'Miami Dream House' pictured in an article from *Pix* magazine. At the time of construction in the post-war period, building materials were still being rationed and, as a result, almost all new buildings were small, single-storey affairs. Keith Perron overcame this minor hurdle by starting his own brickworks company to supply materials for the build. Unfortunately there was no such easy fix for the signature curved glazing, which had to be shipped over from the United Kingdom.

The Perrons' daughter, Judith, had a career in modelling and the house was frequently used for photo shoots. This is a theme that has continued to the present day, with Blue Waters providing the backdrop to several magazine spreads. The house has also played its part in a number of films, most notably Australian film *The Reckoning*, starring Jonathan Lapaglia and Luke Hemsworth, which was shot there in 2014. Much of the interior, which had been painstakingly restored to its original layout by the current owner, has to this day remained as it was on the film set.

Of all the notable guests to frequent the residence over the years, perhaps the most unlikely was a pair of crocodiles brought to the house by the Perrons' two sons after a trip to Darwin. The pond constructed for the crocs remains today, though, fortunately for the neighbours, its inhabitants do not: they eventually decided the time had come to leave Blue Waters and escaped. One was found and donated to Perth Zoo, while the whereabouts of the other remains unknown.

BLUE WATERS

ARCHITECT
Keith D'Alton

CLIENT
Mabel and Keith Perron

YEAR OF COMPLETION
1953

COST
Unknown

STYLE
Inter-war Art Deco

SODA APARTMENTS

19 LINDSAY STREET, PERTH

LINDSAY STREET

SODA APARTMENTS

Rising out of a heritage-listed former Mackay's Aerated Waters factory are the aptly named Soda Apartments. A harmonious relationship between an architect focused on location-specific, functional design and support from a client committed to an innovative, high quality building has led to a wonderful example of genuinely sustainable medium-density housing.

On the narrow site of around 700 square metres, thirteen units have been carefully arranged to optimise orientation and minimise dedicated circulation space. Four of these units are maisonettes, accessed from the first floor with bedrooms facing the laneway on the ground floor. A number of elevated, periscope-like window scoops provide security and privacy while maximising northern light.

The Art Deco–style factory, with its rendered facade on Lindsay Street and industrial face brick wall in the laneway, forms the heavy perimeter out of which the lightweight facade of the apartments emerges. The eye-catching artwork covering the laneway wall formed an integral part of the development proposal, with funding allowing for the work to be refreshed three times. The cladding to the northern wall sits on reverse brick veneer to optimise thermal performance, while the weatherboard profile references the building fabric of the old workers' cottages that are scattered around the precinct. The first floor is set back, creating a shadow zone that allows the upper floors to 'float' above the existing shell and enables old and new to exist in unity.

ARCHITECT
Oldham, Boas & Ednie-Brown (factory); Gresley Abas Architects (new development)

CLIENT
Mackay & Co. Aerated Waters; Private developer

YEAR OF COMPLETION
1928; 2014

COST
Unknown

STYLE
Inter-war Functionalist; Contemporary

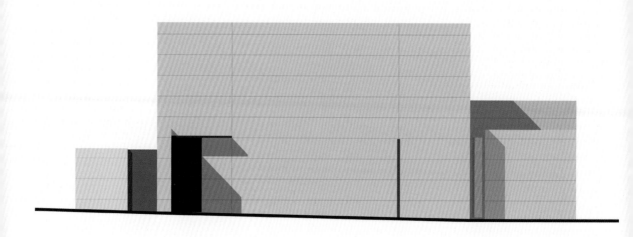

CLOISTER HOUSE

426A CAMBRIDGE STREET, FLOREAT

Every once in a while, a house emerges that becomes a kind of folklore, sparking mystery and intrigue; discussed with gusto at dinner tables and over coffee. Cloister House is one such building.

The foreboding *béton brut*, otherwise known as raw concrete exterior of Cloister House could be interpreted by some as unfriendly, but it is a celebration of the rich and honest texture of formed, or in this case rammed concrete, the contemporary version of the ancient building material of rammed earth. The reason for the absence of street-facing windows is, to put it simply, that the house does not face the street. Instead, it faces in on itself, or rather the large internal courtyard that is somehow squeezed into the middle of the Tardis-like home, which manages to fit itself into the front half of a subdivided lot.

One of the great strengths of the home is how limited its material palette is: concrete and washed timber. The two materials are used in a manner reminiscent of world-famous architect Louis Kahn; masterfully, that is. There is an immense challenge

to filling a home with bespoke solid timber joinery, especially when it is used in lieu of contemporary mass-produced materials and fittings. This challenge has been accepted and accomplished by MORQ, particularly in the bathrooms, which are made entirely from timber and concrete, bar the tapware and basin. The manipulation of natural light is another Kahn trademark that has been interpreted by MORQ. The placement of windows and often unseen gaps in the concrete shell is carefully orchestrated to cause sunlight to dapple off the raw, heavily textured surfaces. Occasionally a deep concrete beam suspended just within arm's reach helps divide a space, begging to be touched. The tranquil courtyard garden that the home is formed around is laden with thriving tropical vegetation that crawls skyward, the cavernous walls reducing the noise of the busy road to a whisper.

Cloister House is the kind of building that divides opinions, but the quality of design and craftsmanship that has gone into this project has resulted in a house that is pushing the boundaries of residential architecture.

CAMBRIDGE STREET

CLOISTER HOUSE

ARCHITECT
MORQ

CLIENT
Private resident

YEAR OF COMPLETION
2017

COST
Unknown

STYLE
Twenty-first Century Brutalist

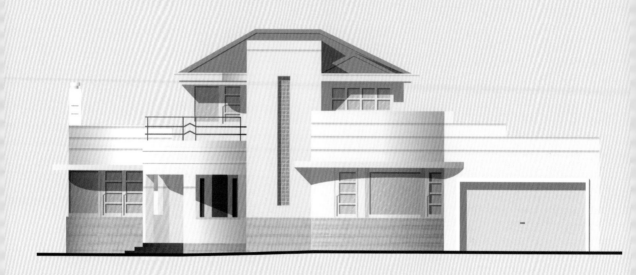

CHISHOLM HOUSE

32 GENESTA CRESCENT, DALKEITH

Designed by one of the early partners of the first privately owned architecture firm in Western Australia, Chisholm House is a much-admired Art Deco delight. Architect Oswald Chisholm, of what is now Cameron Chisholm Nicol, designed the house in 1938 for his family. Following the outbreak of World War II, which saw Chisholm enlist in the Royal Australian Engineers, construction of the house was delayed, with the family not moving in until around 1941. Demonstrating the skill of the designer, the house was the pinnacle of comfort and design for the time, including a sunken backyard conversation pit and a barbecue area that would rival the back patios of today, along with what Chisholm claimed was one of the first internal bathrooms to include a lavatory. Oswald's wife Melva was reportedly aghast at the idea of not placing the throne in the usual spot outide. The Chisholms occupied the luxurious abode until 1961.

An excellent example of the modern styling that was popular during the short-lived construction boom of the late 1930s, the house is fronted by intersecting cylindrical volumes contrasted by a central rectilinear tower. This classic example of Art Deco, reminiscent of Hollywood's golden age, had its brush with the stars when it was used as a location for the 1991 film *Love in Limbo*, featuring a young Russell Crowe.

The suburb of Dalkeith has long been associated with the kind of affluence and style that Chisholm House represents, and is now one of Perth's wealthiest suburbs. This particular area of the affluent and historic suburb of Dalkeith was bought as raw bushland by real estate agents Peet & Co in the early 1900s. Dubbed 'Dalkeith Estate', the neighbourhood was designed in accordance with the 'garden city' movement, with wide, crescent-shaped turns that were intended to accommodate an extension of the nearby Stirling Highway tram line and give the area its much-adored wide-open vistas. In keeping with its genteel theme, its streets were named after yachts racing in the 1912 season – *Cygnet*, *Garland*, *Viking* and *Genesta* to name a few. Those aspirants in the market for a quarter-acre block in the estate, for the modest sum of £35 to £70, were fittingly given a tour in a Gatsby-esque De Dion-Bouton car. Not a bad price to pay considering Chisholm House last sold in 2014 for $2.72 million.

CHISHOLM HOUSE

ARCHITECT
Oswald Victor Chisholm

CLIENT
Oswald Victor Chisholm

YEAR OF COMPLETION
c. 1941

COST
Unknown

STYLE
Inter-war Functionalist / Art Deco

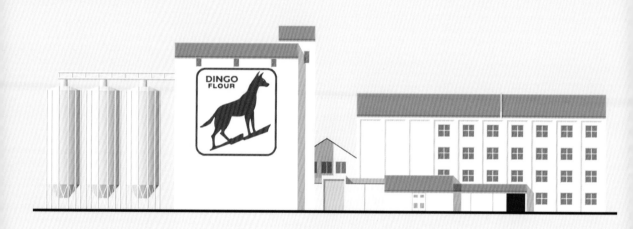

'DINGO' FLOUR MILL

111 STIRLING HIGHWAY, NORTH FREMANTLE

STIRLING HIGHWAY

Since 1940, a four-storey red dingo has welcomed visitors to Fremantle arriving by both land and sea. The logo has become synonymous with the portside town and has made its way onto a host of apparel and artwork, making it an ever-present icon across the city. Contrary to popular belief, the sign wasn't originally painted by Western Australia's infamous businessman Alan Bond during his early years as a sign-writer; the man behind the dingo was in fact Les Nash, who was paid a total sum of £40 for the work. During the Second World War the dingo was painted over, so as to remove the big red bullseye visible to passing planes. In the years since, the sign has been repainted, touched up and even had an eye added, though it remains very faithful to the original design.

The heritage-listed mill on which the image resides is colloquially referred to as the 'Dingo Flour Mill', though it has in fact never been named as such (its actual name, 'Great Southern Roller Flour Mill', doesn't have quite the same ring to it). Built in the Federation Warehouse style, the mill is one of the largest purpose-built mills in the state and is the only remaining mill in operation within the metropolitan area.

The mill was designed by prominent local architect Joseph Francis Allen, whose other works include the East Fremantle Town Hall. The structure of the main rectangular tower that dominates the skyline of the area is made from Norfolk Island pine and clad in metal panels. The Art Deco office building that fronts Stirling Highway was a later addition by the prominent architectural trio of Powell, Cameron & Chisholm, now Cameron Chisholm Nicol.

ARCHITECT
Joseph Francis Allen (mill);
Powell, Cameron & Chisholm (offices)

CLIENT
Great Southern Roller Flour Mills Ltd

YEAR OF COMPLETION
1922; c. 1950

COST
Unknown

STYLE
Federation Warehouse;
Inter-war Art Deco

GLOSSARY

ACADEMIC CLASSICAL STYLE
Mainly seen in large-scale, non-residential architecture. Typically masonry construction with a solid and permanent feel.

ACADEMIC GOTHIC STYLE
Generally asymmetrical masonry buildings adorned with ornamentation and adhering to the medieval structural tradition with materials expressed fairly directly.

ARCHITRAVE
In Classical architecture, the lowest portion of the *entablature*. This can also refer to mouldings surrounding a door or window.

ART DECO STYLE
A style developed in Europe and present in Australia during the inter-war period. Typified by eye-catching materials and finishes, with bold geometric ornamentation.

BAUHAUS STYLE
Influential modernist arts school of the twentieth century, with a key aim to unite fine art with functional design.

BEAUX ARTS STYLE
Present during the inter-war period, with strong ties to the Inter-War Academic Classical style, but with buildings of a larger scale showing more sculptural elements to the facades through the use of classical motifs and detailing.

BRISE-SOLEIL
Projecting elements providing shade from direct sunlight.

BRUTALIST STYLE
Bold, strong shapes, often expressed in concrete or masonry with large areas of ungarnished wall surface.

CANTILEVER
A structural member extending beyond a fulcrum.

CASE STUDY HOUSES
A series of inexpensive and replicable houses built between 1945 and 1966 in the USA, designed by prominent architects of the day to respond to post-war demand.

CHAMFERING
A bevelled surface which is usually cut at 45 degrees to the two adjacent faces.

COLONNADE
A series of equally spaced columns usually supporting one side of a roof structure.

CONTEMPORARY STYLE
Broadly refers to architecture of the present day, can be varied in appearance. The buildings will often show evidence of current technology and sustainable design.

CRENELATED PARAPET
A wall with regularly spaced cutouts for defensive purposes, originating in the Middle Ages. Also called battlements.

DECONSTRUCTIVIST STYLE
Late twentieth century style exploring fragmentation and breaking apart the usual make-up of a building's structure.

ENTABLATURE
In Classical architecture, the structure of mouldings and bands sitting horizontally over the columns, usually composed of *architrave*, *frieze* and *cornice*.

FEDERATION WAREHOUSE STYLE
Links to Romanesque architecture but with limited detailing to the predominantly brickwork facades. Bold features of vertical brick *piers* with strong arches over the top.

FREE CLASSICAL STYLE
A confident style with the language of classical architecture, but used freely with a less rigid approach.

FREE GOTHIC STYLE
Various medieval elements interpreted freely and often exuberantly expressed. A style applied to a wide variety of building types.

FLEMISH BOND
A type of brick pattern with headers (a brick laid with the short side visible) and stretchers (a brick laid with the long side visible) that alternate in each course, with each stretcher having a header above and below it.

FONTHILL GOTHIC
A form of Gothic Revival, Fonthill refers specifically to the architectural elements of Fonthill Abbey in Wiltshire, England.

FRIEZE
The horizontal section between the *architrave* and cornice in the classical *entablature*, often decorated.

FUNCTIONALIST STYLE
Present in Australia's inter-war period, featuring simple geometric forms, often light in colour with large expanses of glass.

GEORGIAN STYLE
Symmetrical buildings featuring repetition, with the proportions of classical architecture, large numbers of

panes to each window sash and typically of masonry construction.

GOTHIC PICTURESQUE STYLE

Buildings often situated in picturesque settings, providing romantic silhouettes. Often random application of medieval motifs and detailing added to fairly simple building forms.

HAMMERBEAM

Used in roof construction. A short horizontal member of the structure which protrudes from the base of the main rafters within a hammerbeam roof.

INTERNATIONAL STYLE

Closely tied to modernism, and typified by repetition of modular forms, large areas of glazing on the facades and minimal use of colour.

MAISONETTE

A small apartment that is part of a larger building, usually over two levels and with its own entrance.

MANSARD ROOF

A roof with a steep slope to the lower portion on all sides and a shallower upper section.

MODERNIST STYLE

A movement based upon the use of new technologies of the early twentieth century – predominantly glass, steel and reinforced concrete – to create simplified forms and clean lines.

NEO-CLASSICAL STYLE

Characterised by grandeur of scale and usually the dramatic use of columns topped with a triangular *pediment*. The buildings typically follow the proportions of Classical architecture.

NOSTALGIC STYLE

Seen in domestic and religious architecture. Typically two-storey buildings that employ a combination of local building methods and those from a given cultural background.

OLD ENGLISH STYLE

A style of 'quaint' residential buildings of the inter-war period in Australia harking back to a romantic ideal of the rural English cottage.

ORGANIC STYLE

Present from the start of Australia's late twentieth century period, showing complex geometry and forms relating to those found in nature.

PEDIMENT

A triangular portion usually at the top and centre of a facade or over a *colonnade*, often decorated.

PIER

Similar to a column but often used to add aesthetic value. Generally don't support horizontal members such as beams and floor slabs.

PLINTH

Base of a column or *pier*, generally square or a continuous structure, often projecting, forming the base of a wall.

PORTICO

A roof covering an entry point to a building, supported by columns.

POSTMODERNIST STYLE

A combination of elements taken from various different styles with strong references to historical architecture and often ornamentation to the facade.

QUOIN

An external corner of a masonry wall, accented through use of a material of a differing colour, texture, size or projection to that of the main wall.

REVEAL

In a door or window opening, the portion of the jamb which is visible between the frame of the door or window and the face of the wall.

ROMANESQUE STYLE

Usually commercial or ecclesiastical buildings. Simple, robust forms, typically with weighty masonry walls.

SECOND EMPIRE STYLE

Dominant roof forms with elegant, crisp detailing. Taking inspiration from French Renaissance architecture.

STRIPPED CLASSICAL STYLE

Sparsely ornamented facades with large areas of plain wall surface. Buildings are usually symmetrical in their massing.

SUN BAFFLE

Another term for a *brise-soleil*.

TOURELLE

A small tower or tower-shaped element projecting from a building.

TUDOR STYLE

Buildings typified by their steep gabled roofs and half-timbered walling with the spaces between the timber filled with stucco or masonry.

WINDOW WALL

Similar to a glazed curtain wall but can be load-bearing and provide structural support.

ACKNOWLEDGEMENTS

This book would undoubtedly not have been possible without the contribution of a number of people and the personal support of others. Tom and Elliot would both like to thank their ever-supportive friends and family, with Elliot making special mention to his much-adored wife Rachel, and Tom to his brilliant friend Valeria who has been a constant source of motivation.

A number of firms and individuals have provided us with drawings and invaluable information on the different buildings of Perth. Their willingness to help and the time they afforded our work has been incredible and very much appreciated. They are listed in no particular order: Ryan Deyonker and Ahmed Abas of Gresley Abas; Adrian Iredale and Narelle Walch of Iredale Pederson Hook; David Cavanagh, owner of Blue Waters; Jordanna Palassis of Palassis Architects; Steven Smyth of Christou Design Group; the staff of the State Library of Western Australia; the staff and curators of Fremantle Prison, especially Assistant Curator Eleanor Lambert; Susan Atkins from the Western Australian Government Department of Planning, Lands and Heritage; and Philip Griffiths of Griffiths Architects.

Lastly, we would like to thank our wonderful publishers at Fremantle Press, who have managed to get a great book out of two people who just liked drawing buildings. Their guidance and continued enthusiasm has made the journey of creating *Built Perth* an enjoyable one.

ABOUT THE AUTHORS

Tom McKendrick made his way over to Australia's west coast having completed a degree in architecture at Northumbria University. For a number of years he worked within various architectural practices in Perth and gained experience across different sectors of the built environment including healthcare, retail, commercial and residential projects. In more recent times, Tom has turned his attention towards his life-long passion of illustration and graphic design, starting his own company in Fremantle.

Elliot Langdon completed a Master of Architecture at the University of Western Australia in 2016. He currently works as an architecture graduate at a Perth-based firm on medium- to large-scale projects in the education, retail, commercial and hospitality sectors. With a keen eye for graphics, design and a passion for writing, Elliot hopes to someday be able to work across multiple creative fields, blurring the lines between architectural, graphic, industrial, and other types of design.

First published 2019 by
FREMANTLE PRESS

Fremantle Press Inc. trading as Fremantle Press
25 Quarry Street, Fremantle WA 6160
(PO Box 158, North Fremantle WA 6159)
www.fremantlepress.com.au

Printed by Everbest Printing Investment Limited, China
Design by Carolyn Brown, tendeersigh.com.au

 A catalogue record for this
book is available from the
National Library of Australia

Built Perth. ISBN 9781925815498 (hardback).

Fremantle Press is supported by the State Government through the
Department of Local Government, Sport and Cultural Industries.

Publication of this title was assisted by the Commonwealth Government
through the Australia Council, its arts funding and advisory body.